Real Alaskans

The author would like to thank the many people who cooperated with their time and their generosity in donating the use of photographs for this book. A special thanks to the Anchorage Daily News for permission to print much of the material contained herein which originally appeared in the pages of that newspaper.

Real Alaskans

Men and Women Who Make the Great Land Great

Lew Freedman

ISBN 0-88839-254-0
Copyright © 1990 Lew Freedman

Cataloging in Publication Data
Freedman, Lew, 1951–
  Real alaskans
  Men and women who make the great land great

  ISBN 0-88839-254-0

  1. Alaska—Biography. 2. Adventure and adventurers—Alaska—Biography. I. Title.

  F903.F74 1990   979.8'05'092   C90-091427-0

All rights reserved. No part of this publication may be reproduced, stored in a retrieval system or transmitted, in any form or by any means, electronic, mechanical, photocopying, recording or otherwise, without the prior written permission of Hancock House Publishers.

The cover artwork for this book was created by Alaskan artist Jon Van Zyle. The painting is entitled "Ah Alaska" and is copyrighted 1987 by Jon Van Zyle. It is reprinted courtesy of Voyageur Art, Minneapolis, Minnesota.

Designed and edited by Herb Bryce
Production by Lorna Lake

Printed in Hong Kong

Published simultaneously in Canada and the United States by

HANCOCK HOUSE PUBLISHERS LTD.
19313 Zero Avenue, Surrey, B.C. V3S 5J9

HANCOCK HOUSE PUBLISHERS
1431 Harrison Avenue, P. O. Box X-1, Blaine, WA 98230

Contents

	Introduction	6
1	Pioneers of the Trail	12
	Susan Butcher	14
	Libby Riddles	26
	DeeDee Jonrowe	39
	Joe Redington	50
	Norman Vaughan	57
2	Old Men and the River	65
	Harry Gaines	67
	Gary Galbraith	77
3	Making Friends with the Snow	82
	Bob Baker	84
	Bill Spencer	93
	Shawn Lyons	117
	John Faeo	127
4	Mountain Highs	135
	Ray Genet	137
	Art Davidson	152
	Harry Johnson	159
5	Through the Eyes of Artists	170
	John Pezzenti	172
	Jon Van Zyle	178
	Fred Machetanz	186
6	Real Alaskans	196
	Jim Okonek	198
	Reggie Joule	208
	George Attla	216

Lew Freedman
Author

Life on the Frontier

When I moved to Alaska from the East Coast of the United States in early 1984, it felt as if I was leaving for a foreign country. On my first vacation back to my old homes of Boston and Philadelphia a little more than a year later, it felt as if I were going to a foreign country.

Maybe that's the definition of a real Alaskan; someone who thinks Alaska is the real world.

Alaska, and particularly Anchorage, its principal city and the hub of the state, is a split vision. It is a soft-focus blur of natural glacial and mountainous wonders that is intensely beautiful; and yet it is also a sharp-focus intrusion of honking horns, spoiled air, and empty storefronts which are remnants of boom-town construction.

You know you've really become an Alaskan when it doesn't faze you that it can cost less to fly to Tokyo than to New York and when it no longer registers that $6.95 for a hamburger is a lot of money.

There are many Alaskas, of course. From Southeast to the North Slope, every region is different. You do have to pass through Anchorage to get to most of them, though. It is said that Anchorage is for people who like the wilderness in small doses. You can see it from there, and drive to it in 20 minutes, but you can also stuff your face at Dairy Queen.

The Outsider's image of Alaska is of a place shrouded in snow and darkness virtually year-round, where everyone lives in igloos or log cabins, where the moose and the grizzly bear play. And that image is certainly fed by things like automobile license plates which read "The Last Frontier."

The new resident's perceptions are altered quickly. The argument can be made that Anchorage has more in common with Philadelphia and Boston than it does with the rest of Alaska. It has McDonald's, condominiums and traffic jams.

Sometimes it is comforting to feel this commonality with the rest of North America. Other times there is a feeling of oppressive distress, that we have blown our last chance not to ruin a corner of the land.

It is nice to have city amenities — grocery stores, movie theatres, live entertainment — but it is disconcerting to realize that the wilderness is just around the corner, tantalizing in its nearness, and that the animal rattling around in the garbage may not be a raccoon, but something with much larger claws.

But for all the ways that Anchorage is not so different from Anywhere, U.S.A., there are an equal number of ways it is unlike the Philadelphias, Fresnos, or Atlantas.

I have never before lived in a city that shoveled snow onto its downtown thoroughfares to start races. The only races I saw run through city streets before were run by humans, not dogs.

Until I lived in a place that features winter from October to nearly April, it hadn't crossed my mind that anyone plugged their car engines into outdoor sockets to keep them warm. In Philadelphia, in a pinch, drivers might park cars next to fire hydrants, but that was not to cool them off.

People who live Outside chuckle at this way of life, but probably their favorite Alaska tales revolve around guns. Think about where you live. You go to the drug store to buy aspirin, toothpaste, maybe school supplies. But not a pistol. That's always been my favorite thing about the local drug store in Anchorage: they may be out of cold cream, but they're never out of firearms.

I found it a trifle surprising when I was moving north to learn that not only did many of my friends have no realistic vision of Alaska, but that neither did they have any real notion of where it was. There were two schools of thought. It was either considered to be so far away that the miles were not computable, or it was thought to be a suburb of Seattle. It is really just about 1,500 air miles from Seattle to Anchorage.

Actually, most Alaskans (especially those from Anchorage, and that's half the population of the state) probably talk tougher than they really are when they send letters home. They may mention in passing that it was minus 52 at Chandalar yesterday—but fail to mention that practically nobody lives around there.

Alaska is a beautiful yet harsh environment and there are lessons that must be learned quickly if you travel away from the downtown business district of Anchorage, particularly if that travel is on foot, and especially if that travel is in the winter.

On the day I arrived in Alaska, a famous Japanese mountain climber named Naomi Uemura became the first man to reach the summit of Mount McKinley in winter by himself. A few days later, on his descent, he disappeared.

It was instructive to watch the evolution of the news bulletins following the incident. One day the story was about how he could be found in a snow cave, or how he might have found cached supplies. The next day he was being written about in the past tense. In other words, after a given period of time, you don't walk off the mountain. If X amount of time has passed, so have you.

One other unique aspect of living in Alaska: a person gets used to the most incredible natural phenomena, the types of things you only used to read about in National Geographic. Things like volcanic eruptions. And earthquakes.

Mount Redoubt on the Kenai Peninsula, some 150 miles south of Anchorage, began blowing off steam in December, 1989, and many months later it hadn't completely cooled off. In the beginning, the falling ash disrupted air traffic, in some instances grounding jets. As long as there is no interference in daily life, we don't pay that much attention to other eruptions.

My first noticeable earthquake occurred when I was deep in conversation in a bicycle store. It took us a moment to realize that the shimmy we felt was not from a passing gravel truck, but from a 5.7 quake. The bicycles on the racks vibrated like tuning forks for more than a minute.

My first glimpse of the Northern Lights shamed any psychedelic concert of the 1960s.

A huge expanse of sky was lighted by shimmering curtains of yellowish light, some glowing and fading, some spreading. In wispy thin lines like skywriting. There were a million stars visible between the darting lights. I watched on and off for an hour.

In most cities, bicyclists and drivers must swerve to avoid dogs. In Anchorage a few years ago a small bear ran across the road during a bicycle race. And it's the rare driver who hasn't been startled by the threat of a moose crossing the highway.

A person who lives in Anchorage and doesn't venture outside the city limits, either to hike in the near Chugach Mountains, to fish the Kenai River, to explore the Matanuska-Susitna Valley, may not earn the right to call himself a real Alaskan. And even that committed, mobile, and active person may only be skimming the surface of Alaska. There are few places to go for day drives, few roads.

But if you live in Anchorage, what do you do, get on a single-engine plane and fly into the Bush to look at an Eskimo village for a half hour and say you've seen it? Even if you go, where do you stay? There aren't any Hiltons at Anaktuvuk Pass.

You can have your Alaska many ways and people make their choices. Many of the people I have come to know who make their home in Alaska have made the choice to challenge Alaska, to wrestle with it, take it on when it comes head on in a bad mood.

One of Alaska's nicknames is The Great Land. The appellation is earned in two ways. Alaska is the Great Land both because it is huge — by far the largest state in the country — and because it is great in what it has to offer. And what that includes is Mount McKinley, the highest mountain on the North American continent at 20,320 feet; wild, raging rivers; wilderness you can get lost in, and untamed beauty.

The men and women who first challenged Alaska's rugged terrain came as explorers and settlers. Those who settled and who have watched technology and modernization follow have found new challenges. Those are the people who are the stars of this book. Whether they are dog mushers, mountain climbers, skiers, or artists, they are people who are at one with the country. They are trying to reach back to the past and preserve it both in how they live today and for the future.

That truly is what they have in common, what their stories are about. Alaska can be tough, but Alaskans can be tougher, might be their motto.

Just ask Susan Butcher, Bob Baker or George Attla. These are some of the people you will meet in these pages. These are some of the people who understand that Alaska is a place of great beauty, enormous contrasts, and daring adventures. They don't take their Alaska sitting down.

Lew Freedman is sports editor of the Anchorage Daily News, in Anchorage, Alaska. He grew up in Boston, Massachusetts, and has degrees from Boston University and Alaska Pacific University.

A journalist all of his adult life, Mr. Freedman has won more than fifty awards for his writing, about sports, the outdoors, and other topics. He has also worked as a political reporter and has had articles appear in such prestigious publications as *Summit Magazine, Ring Magazine,* and the *New York Times.*

In addition, Mr. Freedman was honored with a profesional teaching fellowship in 1990 at Colorado State University.

Mr. Freedman, his wife Donna, and their daughter Abby make their home in Anchorage.

He is the author of *Dangerous Steps,* the story of Vernon Tejas's solo winter ascent of Mount McKinley.

1

Pioneers of the Trail

For nearly two weeks each March, normal business in much of the state of Alaska is interrupted. People may go to work, but they make phone calls, turn on the radio or television quite frequently. They all have the same question: Who's ahead in the Iditarod Trail Sled Dog Race?

The race is a throwback to wilderness Alaskan roots, even for residents who wouldn't dare to drive their cars outside of the city in winter. It is both sporting event and spiritual renewal and fans most definitely have their favorites in the 1,100-plus-mile race from downtown Anchorage to the city of Nome. It is a rugged race and the mushers can face inhuman weather and dangerous trail obstacles ranging from moose to blizzards.

In recent years, the Iditarod has become the symbol of something else: women's equality. In few sports do women compete head-to-head with men; in fewer, best them. Since 1985, women's victories have almost been the norm.

When Libby Riddles became the first woman ever to win the event, women everywhere were proud. They became prouder still in 1986 when Susan Butcher began her domination of this tough, demanding endurance challenge. Butcher has won the race a record-equaling four times; not many would bet against her winning a record-setting fifth. And not to be overlooked is DeeDee Jonrowe, who seems poised to emerge as a champion of the future.

You don't have to be a winner to earn the respect and cheers of the fans in the cities and villages along the trail. Not at all. Some spectators bundle themselves against the cold merely to wait until the old-timers come along. Joe Redington, a co-founder of the Iditarod, has his fan club, and everyone roots for Norman Vaughan, who has been mushing dogs for over 60 years and is now in his 80s.

Every musher in the Iditarod has a great personal adventure. Every musher has a worthwhile story to tell. These are the stories of five of those mushers.

Susan Butcher
of Eureka

The Driven Lady of the Iditarod Trail

Susan Butcher's world is a dog yard in the Interior of Alaska. On most days of the year, most hours of the day, she talks to more dogs than people.

On most days of the year, most hours of the day, she breeds dogs, feeds dogs, runs dogs. She does not eat until they eat. She does not sleep until they sleep.

On most days of the year, most hours of the day, there is no time for reading, no time for music, no time for television, telephone chat, movies, or vacations. Fifteen hours a day, seven days a week, there is only time for dogs.

She does not miss people, or play.

"There is no problem with me being a workaholic still," says Butcher. "I was born that way. I'm made that way. I enjoy it. I'm all-consumed by it, but it doesn't bother me. I don't miss anything else I could be doing with my time. I love dog mushing."

In Susan's world, the dogs reign. She holds their paws when they are sick all night sometimes, which she did with her favorite leader Granite. She gives them all the energy a body can muster. She asks only that they run for her.

They do.

Four times Susan Butcher's dogs have run faster than anyone else's. They won three straight Iditarod Trail Sled Dog races in 1986, 1987, and 1988, and then a fourth in 1990 after finishing second in 1989. She has won big money — over $200,000 in purses in that time — and set record after record, both on the northern route and the southern route on the Iditarod Trail, covering the 1,100 or so miles in just over 11 days.

The dogs age, the dogs change, but there are always fast dogs to take their places. There are 150 to choose from in Butcher's kennel.

Only Butcher, the musher, stays the same.

Champions don't repeat. You hear that all the time in professional sports. They win once and lose the hunger. They win once and sate their hunger on the banquet circuit.

Susan Butcher is different. She repeats.

"One of the main things people have to do to repeat is not think, 'I've got it in the bag,' " says Butcher.

She has shown no signs of relaxing, no signs of finding the work it takes to succeed at dog mushing to be tedious or repetitious.

"I believe what we see Susan doing is what should be happening," says perennial Iditarod contender Jerry Austin of St. Michael. "We're seeing the person who's putting in the most effort have the work rewarded.

"I think we have to realize here with Susan Butcher that it's her job and she views it as a job. Just about everyone else is a working stiff."

Butcher will go to the occasional banquet — say to pick up the Women's Sports Foundation's Professional Sportswoman of the Year award that she has won twice — but she can still get lost. It is easy to get lost in Eureka, 140 miles northwest of Fairbanks. She lives in a cabin there with husband Dave Monson, a few handlers, her huskies, and 10,000 trees for company.

Usually, this is Butcher's retreat once winter settles in, but at times she has been forced out of the fortress by extreme weather. In late January of 1989 when the subzero cold swept across Alaska and the thermometer hit 73 degrees below (Fahrenheit) at her home, she was pushed into exile. Butcher, Monson, and 48 dogs fled south to Willow, 75 miles north of Anchorage, to fellow musher DeeDee Jonrowe's house. Butcher is driven, not crazy.

"Usually, the southcentral mushers come up to our place because they have no snow, so it evens out," says Butcher.

The network of trails leading from Jonrowe's yard allows a musher the freedom to roam the backcountry for days without covering the same ground. Sometimes during that '89 cold snap, Butcher harnessed up and disappeared for long runs, camping overnight in the cold. She loves her dogs, true, but she also loves the country, where it is unspoiled and solitude fills the night. She has yet to tire of that.

Butcher recounts a 100-mile run.

"It was what a lot of people would call miserable," she says, "It was cold, but I didn't think it was miserable. I get as cold as the next person. My back gets a little bit sore, but I enjoy it. As I do it, I think, 'This will help me win the Iditarod. This is worth it.' Then I feel good about it."

Butcher was sitting in the waiting room of the Bering Sea Animal Clinic, waiting on a sick dog. She was dressed for dog work in a thick, green jersey, pale green pants, and work boots. Her long, brown hair was tied behind her head. As she spoke, she motioned with her hands frequently to emphasize points and her eyes flashed alternately with intensity and bemusement as she considered questions.

She has certain looks. If you have ever seen Butcher in the cold with her dogs, her cheeks flushed red from the frost, you have seen her at her best, filled with joy. At other times she seems almost defiant. Perhaps that is a remnant of the days when she considered the Iditarod a men's club that had no warmth for women. She seems mellower now.

Jonrowe, who has finished in the top 10 of the Iditarod three times, thinks Butcher is misunderstood and considers her a good friend.

"I'm not sure that people really know her for the quality of person she is," says Jonrowe. "She's very compassionate."

Butcher is in her mid-30s, but it is clear she is not tired of winning. Why should she be? It took so long for the girl who grew up hating the city in Cambridge, Massachusetts, to find Alaska. Then it took so long to win one Iditarod.

Butcher did her first Iditarod in 1978, three years after coming to the state, and by 1980 was in the top five. She finished second in 1982 and 1984 and everyone knew victory was coming. It seemed inevitable that Butcher would be the first woman to win the Iditarod, but in 1985 she had to withdraw because her team was stomped by a moose and Libby Riddles took that honor.

The ensuing five years made up for that disappointment, yet Butcher insists her early races didn't discourage her.

"It wouldn't have been the end of the world if I'd never won," says Butcher. "It wasn't like I didn't enjoy my second-place finishes. People said I was always a loser finishing second, but I looked at it as "Hey, I'm one step away from winning.' "

Winning can change a person. If they have sweated hard for a goal and reach it, they can feel let down — or they can fight that very human of tendencies. Butcher has fought it. Iditarod winners get fancy trophies and Butcher kept the first one in the house. She kept the second one in the house, too. But when she won a third, she cleared them all out, put them in the dog barn.

"I'd feel it was detrimental to go into a race thinking, 'I'm the three-time champion and you guys have to beat me,' " says Butcher.

You have to wonder what drives Butcher after all these years, though. Winning again and again has never been enough. All of it has been great, all of it has been special, but none of it has been enough.

Butcher had hinted that she would take time off from the Iditarod once she lost, which she did in 1989, but within moments of her finish, standing under the burled arch that is the finish line on Front Street in Nome, she seemed to have forgotten that idea. She had just finished second to Joe Runyan of Nenana and retirement wasn't the first thing that came to mind. Getting her crown back was.

"Joe's put out a challenge I've got to beat," she said at that time.

And a year later she did so.

Defeat, however, was almost as important to the Butcher image as victory had been. Butcher is so driven, such a workaholic, that she can be short with people, particularly if she is under pressure. At the end of the 1989 race, she was under pressure of a different sort. She was the expected winner and she hadn't finished as the winner. She had also functioned for 11 days on little sleep, so all the ingredients for testiness were there.

We come to know our champions through their victories, but we also come to understand champions by the way they handle stress. A champion may be proud, but not arrogant, or risk public wrath. A champion can be dignified loser, not a sore one, or risk public scorn.

Sometimes an athlete can make more friends in losing honorably than in winning easily.

The 1989 race was a tough one for Butcher to swallow. She came into it with extraordinary confidence, convinced she was mushing behind the best team she'd ever had. And then illness swept through the dogs, making them sick, forcing some of them out of the race, slowing the others.

Butcher said that she knew for the last 150 miles that there was no way she could catch Runyan, but that didn't mean she wouldn't make a game try. She lost to him by slightly over an hour.

Crossing the finish line on a sunny afternoon in the old gold rush town on the Bering Sea coast, Butcher smiled. She didn't cry and she didn't mourn. She insisted she was happy with second place.

It was a critical moment for her. Some of her competitors have accused Butcher of being a hard woman who can snap at others. Here, in front of a crowd of thousands, a poor response to defeat could have soiled the memory of her victories, could have dissolved the warmth of fans who waved signs of support and shouted, "We love you." "Hey, Susan, you're No. 1."

There are so many fair-weather athletes who love the public in victory and snarl and hide when they lose. This wasn't Butcher. Not at all. She grinned and said all the right things to, perhaps, even win the hearts of detractors.

"I am very proud of Joe Runyan," she said.

It was enough. Later, Butcher explained her attitude.

"There was a lot of happiness in coming in second as opposed to tenth," she said. "And I don't believe in sore losers. It wasn't Joe Runyan's fault, or anyone else's fault. Luck is luck. Who is to blame? There is no reason for me to be sour at anybody."

The graciousness didn't mean, however, that Butcher wasn't already thinking of ways to win again. If there was no rest for a champion, think of how little free time there would be for an ex-champion.

Butcher redoubled her training, made more hours in the day. This most focused of athletes has gone two months without picking up her mail and long spells without claiming her phone messages. She went through another year—that made 11 years—without a vacation.

And when March, 1990, came, Butcher was there in Anchorage, ready to start the run to Nome, ready to capture the crown again. Was this team better than the one that was so special in 1989?

"You absolutely have to improve every year," says Butcher. "And not by inches. We're at the limits of what our dog teams can do, but not at the limit of each individual dog. We just have more of them that are good."

In Butcher's case, that means very good indeed.

Just about everyone says Butcher has the best dogs. And lots of them. So many that husband Dave Monson could run the second team in the Yukon Quest, 1,000 miles between Fairbanks and Whitehorse, Yukon Territory, and win it in 1988.

It is like breeding thoroughbreds. After time and Butcher has been doing this for more than a decade bloodlines tell.

Musher Martin Buser of Big Lake, who has finished as high as third in the Iditarod, marvels at Butcher's huge dog lot. "She's cranking out pups year after year and she uses the best of the best," says Buser. "Playing the numbers game is the way to do it." Butcher keeps the best dogs for herself and leases or sells the others.

"How can we beat Susan when the dogs she is selling us are better than what we're running?" asks Jerry Austin. "That says a lot to me right there."

If there were any doubts about how much depth resides in the Butcher team, she answered those questions forever during the winter of 1990.

In January, Butcher raced the Kobuk 220 in Kotzebue, Alaska, the John Beargrease Sled Dog Marathon in Minnesota, and the Kuskokwim 300 in Bethel, Alaska. She won the first two in record time and finished second in the Kusko. With three different teams. Butcher must have the most athletic pets in America outside of Claiborne Farms, breeders of Kentucky Derby caliber horses.

How could Butcher not feel confidence in the team that mushed out of Anchorage on the trail to Nome for the 1990 race? As it turned out, though, injuries that left some dogs limping and illness that struck again, knocked four of her top leaders out of the race in the first 400 miles. She was down to 13 dogs when other leaders had as many as 18.

"It was just a real shock," says Butcher.

One of the dogs Butcher had to leave at a checkpoint was Granite, the most special of her leaders and three times a champion. Granite was nine years old by race time and Butcher so wanted to make him a four-time champion.

Last year, when Butcher felt she was driving her best-ever team, she wondered if Granite would make the cut.

"It's possible Granite will retire before the race," said Butcher then. "If so, it's only because he got bumped by someone better and younger. I want to take Granite out of sentimentality. He's my best friend. It's nice to have your best friend on the trail."

In the end, Butcher took Granite on the trail in 1989, and again in 1990 — out of sentimentality. But there is no room for sentiment in big money competitions, so when it became clear Granite couldn't race to Nome, Granite went into the basket and out of the race.

And yet the Butcher team regrouped around new leaders who had never been asked to take on such responsibility. They regrouped and ran fast—faster than anyone else—and when the race was over, Butcher not only had her fourth Iditarod trophy, she also had a new record time of 11 days, 1 hour, 53 minutes.

The dogs had performed in ways even Butcher hadn't counted on. They had learned to be leaders under fire. Clearly, Butcher's instincts about them had been right from the time they were chosen from the litter to be racing dogs.

Judging talent, that's what it's about. When a Butcher pup runs for the first time it is being watched, evaluated, not based on the sheen of its coat, or even the speed of its feet. What Butcher wants to see is heart. She wants to know that the dog has the same inner drive to run that she has, and a love of racing.

"You can certainly teach them to love it, if you love it," says Butcher, "and you can't have a handler do it. It has to be personal. They get a lot of Susan."

Quite a lot of Susan. If the dog will run for her, Butcher will run for the dog. She once ran to the clinic with a dog showing signs of infection, ditching her plans for the day to babysit him.

"She never quits," says Bob Sept. The former chief veterinarian of the Iditarod, Sept runs Bering Sea Animal Clinic and he has known Butcher for a dozen years.

"She has always had that intensity and real attention for detail."

A standard prerace vet check for a dog consists of heart, lungs, and color of urine tests. It takes a half hour. But checking Butcher's team takes four hours, says Sept.

"We'll check every toenail, check every tooth," he says.

Why? Because she wants to change the odds in the race, says Butcher. "I think, 'I'm a musher, you guys are all mushers. We've all got an equal chance, so I'd better work my ass off to unequalize it.' "

Four Iditarod championships. Besides Butcher, only Rick Swenson of Two Rivers, near Fairbanks, has done that. Swenson won in 1977, 1979, 1981, and 1982. He has finished second three other times.

Swenson and Butcher have spit fire at each other, though Swenson did have a place of honor at Butcher's 1985 wedding, indicating relations weren't always so tense. In 1988, near the end of the race, Swenson said he thought a lot of Alaskans would be pretty happy to see someone besides Butcher win for a change. He hasn't enjoyed reading "Alaska: Where Men Are Men and Women Win The Iditarod" T-shirts.

Butcher, though, has never said there is anything special to her about matching Swenson. She has always said that winning four is what you have to do before you can win a record five times. Five is the number on her mind.

What it will take for Butcher to be satisfied, if anything will satisfy her, is to win the Iditarod five times and to win it in 10 days. Break the victory record and the time barrier.

"Those are the goals I've set for myself," says Butcher.

Can she do it? Probably, if nothing interferes.

Before one recent Iditarod, Jerry Austin laughed when he was asked what he thought of the chances of beating Butcher.

"We were all kind of hoping she'd get pregnant this summer," he replied.

Not a farfetched hope, actually. Butcher knows that to have kids, she would have to change her training habits and probably skip the Iditarod for a year or more.

"I do want to have children," she confirms.

There is no age limit rule in mushing, and no rule of thumb, either. Many of the top mushers are in their mid-30s. Runyan is in his 40s. Joe Redington, Jr., the Father of the Iditarod, is in his 70s and he's still a top contender. There's no reason why Butcher can't take a break and after maternity leave come back and be a champion again. Probably only her mental outlook would be a barrier. If she can recover her intensity after taking time off, she could be a threat to win all over again.

That drive is what propels Butcher. She has never let it flag and one way she has done so is by living in isolation in the bush.

Whenever she emerges from her hamlet, she is an object of curiosity, a celebrity accorded celebrity attention. She is perhaps the most recognizable living Alaskan.

Just moving through the Anchorage International Airport from checkin to gate earlier this year, Butcher was recognized by ticket agents, security guards, and passers-by. As soon as she sat down at her gate, a man walked up to her and exclaimed, "Sue Butcher, I want to shake your hand. Good luck in that Iditarod."

Later, a woman who was also waiting for the flight approached and said, "I just have to tell you what a terrific role model you are."

Butcher smiled and thanked her for saying so. That happens all the time, Butcher said when the woman left.

Those are the kinds of distractions Butcher seeks to avoid most of the time and which she can avoid when she is back home in her dog lot, running dogs on a wooden cart on the dirt in summer, or running them in the woods.

Butcher knows, of course, that she can't hide in the bush all the time. People seek her out. She is showered with awards and it would be rude to say she is too busy to come to Europe to accept.

"We turn down every offer we possibly can," she says. "But it's good for the sport. If you want it to grow, that's the pressure I have being a spokesperson in the sport."

However, Butcher will never let even extraordinary recognition such as her 1990 visit to the White House to meet President George Bush interfere with her training. She knows that if she wants to win that fifth Iditarod, to go faster than any dog team has ever run before, she can't skimp on training.

Once, Butcher said that actually racing the Iditarod, over the frozen ground, in horrendous cold, into fierce winds, is a vacation for her. Then all of the distractions have been peeled away. No one is calling asking her to do anything. She is out there alone on the trail, just her and her dogs.

Those are the moments she prizes most. Those are the moments when all of Alaska is transformed into Susan Butcher's dog yard.

Libby Riddles
of Banner Creek

Princess of the Iditarod

Mommy is here to visit. The dogs scream with delight.

Standing in the middle of a wire mesh pen in the yard behind her Banner Creek cabin, Libby Riddles grins joyfully as baby huskies jump all over her.

"You guys got no manners at all," Riddles admonishes this pack of happy animals. "What are you doing? You think I'm a human ladder, don't you?"

The dogs yip. They nip at her fingers. They bark incessantly, like impatient drivers hammering on their horns at rush hour.

Libby Riddles, her blonde hair blowing freely and cheeks flushed from the chilly October wind, is radiant in the fading afternoon sun, playing with her dogs.

If Susan Butcher is the Queen of the Iditarod, then Libby Riddles is the Princess.

Butcher is the best long-distance musher in the world these days. No arguments. Four wins in the 1,100-mile Iditarod Trail Sled Dog Race from Anchorage to Nome, all in record time, prove it.

But Libby (you say Libby in Alaska and people know who you're talking about) did something Butcher couldn't, did something no one can ever take away from her. In 1985, she became the first woman to win the Iditarod.

The way that she did it stirred the imagination of the country. She sprinted out of Unalakleet, the tiny Arctic village on the Bering Sea coast, into howling, subzero winds while the men chose to stay put. When the storm closed in, she was forced to survive the night in her sled bag. But when she awoke the next morning to calm, Riddles had an insurmountable lead.

There was definitely Libbymania out there. TV talk shows and book contracts beckoned. Magazines as varied as Vogue and Sports Illustrated published long accounts of her victory. The national Women's Sports Foundation named her Professional Athlete of the Year. Suddenly, people who wouldn't have known the Iditarod from the Isthmus of Panama were calling.

"How she did it is far more important to the race than that she was the first woman," said Leo Rasmussen, president of the Iditarod Trail Committee. "Was Libby's win important? To tell you that it wasn't would be telling you the greatest lie on earth."

Much time has passed since Riddles zoomed from a musher in the middle of the pack to one of the best-known Alaskans in the world, but she always seemed somewhat perplexed by the Libby Phenomenon.

Sitting in her kitchen sipping coffee, she shook her head. "I still don't know what to make of it," she said. "It's pretty amazing. Oh yeah, it's been wonderful. Ninety-nine point nine percent wonderful."

Sports drama creates instant heroes, but they can often be quickly discarded. Sports are very much a what-have-you-done-for-me-lately world.

Riddles earned her fame with her victory in 1985, but Libby didn't race the 1986 Iditarod because it was her then-partner Joe Garnie's turn to run the dogs. She dropped out of the 1987 race. And she didn't start the 1988 race because she didn't think she could handle racing the first Alpirod International Sled Dog Race in Europe in January and the Iditarod in March, too. Instead, she did commentary for ABC-TV.

In 1989, Riddles, with her own kennel, finished 16th, but then in 1990 she wasn't able to race at all again. Surgery on an injured hip kept her sidelined for the whole mushing season.

That means Riddles has only finished one Iditarod since she won it. So what have you done for us lately, Libby?

Ask her that, and Libby's cheeks flush a darker shade of red than they do in the biting wind. Just because she didn't make the run between Anchorage and Nome every year doesn't mean she was in hibernation. After all, she was third in the Alpirod in 1988, racing village to village through Europe. That should count for something.

"It makes it sound like I was knitting all winter," Riddles said of the way some people viewed her time off.

Banner Creek is a suburb of Nome. Or as much of a suburb as a place with eight people can be. There are a mess of dogs. Libby has more than 50 of them, all part of Blazing Kennels.

In late October, the nearby ground remains clear of snow. From the home she helped build with her own hands, Libby sees rising hillocks, some topped with the first dusting of snow. Below their crests run acres of browning grass.

There are no trees, only naked bushes. The sun is bright in the clear, blue sky, and the wind is just strong enough to make the 20-degree temperature bothersome.

Inside, the musher of the house reclines in a chair at the kitchen table wearing a non-matching sweat shirt and sweat pants. Above her head, on a shelf, is a glass bowl with two goldfish, which Libby suggests could be the ugliest goldfish in America. At least the one belonging to her dog handler Kelly Krueger, a high school senior from Minnesota. One of these days, Danger, Libby's cat, and the beast that is truly in charge here, might reach down and pluck one from the water. Given that the cat is surrounded by bigger, potentially hostile dogs, Danger definitely has an attitude. Sometimes, says Libby, she's not sure Danger realizes he's a cat.

Books are sprinkled on other shelves, and some trophies, too. The huge cup she earned for winning the Iditarod has vines growing out of it. No, she didn't plant crops in there. The plant and its dirt are safely encased in a planter within the cup. But it's certainly an attention getter.

Libby is talking about her favorite subject: dogs. In particular, lead dogs. The lead dog for a top-notch sled-dog racing team must be as smart as the quarterback of a football team or the point guard of a basketball team. Sometimes smarter, since the dog's instinct and the direction it chooses in blowing snow on a pitch-black night can be the difference between winning and losing—even life and death.

The best mushers are no better than their best dogs. When Libby won the Iditarod in 1985, her main leaders were Dugan and Axle. These days, Axle, 9, is retired from racing and spends as much time in the house as he does in the yard. Axle is a ham. He has experience posing with Libby for pictures. When she jokes that he only wants to be photographed from his best side, darned if Axle doesn't turn to the right.

Dugan is still the king of the yard. And the biggest stud. Only one of the dogs aren't related to him. Only three weren't raised by Libby.

"I'm pretty proud of that," she says between bites of a lunch of peanut butter and green apples.

Dugan, 9, remains able despite his age. He was still part of the team in 1989, Libby's last Iditarod. He is the standard by which others are measured.

"It's hard for me to believe that I'll ever drive a dog like him again," says Libby. "Some dogs are just once-in-a-lifetime dogs."

The process of choosing leaders begins early. Each spring—after the Iditarod—Libby starts running her dogs. Over the next few months she narrows the number of racing prospects to 24. Before the 1989 race, she had about 30 with racing experience. Those dogs were from 2 to 7 years old.

In 1988, when Libby split up with boyfriend and partner Garnie and moved from Teller to Banner Creek, she got half of the dogs she used to win the 1985 Iditarod. That meant there were plenty of openings on the first team.

"I just like to get good experience on them," says Libby. "I usually don't try them in lead until their second season."

The dog that shows signs of being a potential leader will be a solid 45-to-60-pound animal who responds well to commands, knows how to keep the line taut, and doesn't tangle the harness.

"The truth is, I like to try just about all of my dogs in lead at one time or another, because you get the darndest surprises," she says.

One member of the friskiest members of the team would be sent to the principal's office all the time if it were a kid. Paligator, who, Libby says, behaves like an escapee from a canine psycho ward, chases anything that moves.

"I had to convince him he couldn't eat any cross-country skiers," says Libby.

Riddles says many of these kinds of things deadpan. She jokes about running the Alpirod with a team of pit bulls: "You don't want to pass that Riddles team."

Libby guards her innermost feelings closely, but when she lets them, her blue eyes twinkle with mischief. Such as when she abruptly picks up a toy plane and dive-bombs the fish bowl.

"Goldfish torture," she quips.

Winning the Iditarod changed Libby's life. She won $50,000. She earned respect. She was in demand.

Sponsors came to her instead of her scrambling to muster the $1,249 Iditarod entry fee. Life became easier than it was when subsistence fishing helped feed the dogs and she raised money by sewing fur hats.

Those are tangible things. But the win changed something inside Libby as well. Friends can see it.

"I think any of us would change when you have a victory of that magnitude," says musher DeeDee Jonrowe of Willow. "She has a lot more confidence, a lot more awareness of self. I think it's definitely left some confidence in her, and I think that's great."

Libby does not dispute the observation.

"I'd be crazy to deny that," she says, "though sometimes it's harder to see that in yourself."

Libby—christened Elizabeth, but don't dare call her that—was raised in Wisconsin, Washington, and Minnesota as the daughter of a college professor. She came to Alaska 18 years ago from St. Cloud with musher Dewey Halverson. After they broke up, she lived in a cabin in Nelchina for a couple of years. From there she moved to Teller, 70 miles north of Nome. From there to Banner Creek.

"This is the first place I've lived in Alaska where I could have a shower every night," she says.

In Banner Creek, she has her own electrical generator and can watch television. Still, she says of these open spaces, "There aren't any 7-11s."

Before 1985, Libby had run the Iditarod twice. She finished 18th in 1980 and 20th in 1981. Between 1981 and 1985, she raced shorter events and gained experience, and with Garnie bred a better team. When she harnessed her dogs in '85, she knew she had a team that could contend.

"I had high hopes for this pack of mutts," Libby wrote in *Race Across Alaska,* the book she coauthored with Tim Jones. "I thought these dogs could even win the race if I could handle them right."

The funny thing is, tons of things went wrong from the beginning in the 1985 race. Who would have guessed they would turn out so right?

On the first day out from Anchorage, she snapped the brake on her sled. Then the dogs wrapped themselves around a tree. When she freed them, they got away and dragged her on her face as she tried to hold on to them. A couple of days later, she took a fall, somersaulting over the sled and smashing a finger. The knuckle was damaged, the finger swelled, and she couldn't take the ring off her finger for a year. Later in the race, she fell asleep on the back of the sled and cracked her head on a tree branch.

And those were the minor annoyances. Libby won the race by risking her life on the trail at 52-below between Unalakleet and Shaktoolik.

People applauded the audacity of her move. Rather than sit out the storm in comfort in Unalakleet, she rode into the wind. All of her pursuers, thinking her foolhardy, made camp.

Libby has relived the moment of her decision and her night of fear in the arctic cold many times since. The determination of the moment lives on in the firmness of her voice.

"You get in that situation and you deal with it," she says. "I was in that race to do my damned best, and that storm was not going to get in the way. I was mentally prepared to do anything within the realm of sanity to keep moving forward. It was going to be scary, but I was confident I could do it without panicking."

When the race was nearly over and first place was secured a mere fifteen miles from Nome, Libby heard Hobo Jim singing "The Iditarod Song" on the radio she carried in her sled. They were playing her song.:

> *I just pulled out of Safety;*
> *I'm on the trail all alone*
> *I'm doing fine and picking up time*
> *And running into Nome*
> *There's no sled tracks in front of me.*
> *And no one else on my tail*
> *I did, I did, I did the Iditarod Trail.*

Libby listened with tears streaming down her cheeks, and when she crossed the finish line and someone asked her how she felt, she said, "What I feel is, if I died right now, it'd be OK."

Libby's win not only changed Libby, it also changed America's view of the Iditarod.

"It was a real turning point," said Bob Sept, former Iditarod Trail Committee president.

Before Libby's win, he said, the public outside the state had a vague notion there was a long sled dog race in Alaska. After her win, "they knew the name of the race."

The impact of the victory as a barrier breaker can't be underestimated. Libby had never been a contender before she won. The dominant woman was Butcher. Butcher had finished second, and it was understood that it was just a matter of time until she won, an assumption firmly proven correct in the ensuing years. The year Libby won was the year Butcher withdrew after her team was stomped by a moose.

When Libby, not she, became the first woman to win the race, Butcher was at first depressed.

"I was beat by a moose," said Butcher, who said her victories since have more than made up for the feeling of loss she had at the time. "That made it really tough for me."

For mushers like Jonrowe, who has finished the Iditarod eight times with a best finish of third, watching Libby win was living vicariously.

"I wanted to see a woman win the race, whichever one of us it was," said Jonrowe. "Susan had made quite a dent, but it showed there were women, not just one woman, competing in the race. That was significant. Susan was thought of as an anomaly."

If Libby had any doubts about whether her achievement touched the masses, they were dispelled when she became the spokesperson for the Alaska Chapter of the American Lung Association's antismoking campaign in 1985 and 1986. The second year, Libby spoke to some 5,000 students from elementary to high school age.

Deborah Williams, then executive director of the local chapter, remembers what it was like.

"It was really quite extraordinary," said Williams. "You saw hero worship, and you don't see that very much in Alaska. They'd run up to her for autographs, to touch her."

Reminded of her post-race comment about being happy enough to die right then and there, Libby blushed.

"It just kind of came right out," she said.

As Libby marches out the door of her house wearing a bright red windsuit and a leather hat with flaps that make her look like Amelia Earhart, the dogs in the lot rise as one and bark with excitement. Tethered to poles next to the small square boxes that are their shelters, they recognize what's going on here as she announces, "Hey, you huskies."

Some of them will get to run and they seem to bark, "Take me! Take me!"

It is still early in the season. With no snow covering the dusty dirt road that passes Libby's house, the dogs will pull Libby straddling a four-wheeler. This will be a half-hour run, but it takes nearly that long for Libby and handler Kelly Krueger to harness the team one by one. The frenzied dogs must be gripped tightly by the collar and hauled to the 40-foot line in front of the vehicle, then tied in even as they jump with anticipation. Libby has long, sturdy fingers and thick forearms. She needs them for this kind of work.

The dogs bark, their tongues hang out of their mouths, and they strain at their harnesses. Libby beams, unconsciously deriving pleasure from the sight of these thoroughbreds and their eagerness to run. When she climbs up on the seat and releases the brake, they explode as if a starter's pistol has been fired. The dogs burst into full stride — zero to 60 in no time at all — and then settle into a trot.

They wind around a curve in the road trailing clouds of dust. Libby shouts "Haw!" and the team turns left onto the main road that leads to Nome. A few hundred yards further down the road she yells "Gee!" and the team turns right onto the property of a neighbor who doesn't mind the dog training.

Eventually, she directs her dogs to a gravel pit with water that is partially frozen. They stick their noses into it and drink what they can. Then it's a quick run home.

As soon as she is parked, Libby and Krueger ladle a thin broth into dishes to feed the dogs.

"Drink, guys," says Libby.

But Paligator wants more than his share and initiates antisocial behavior. Libby gets stern. "You know better, don't you?" Paligator still acts up. "Sometimes — dang it."

One by one as she brings them back to their little houses, Libby coos to her dogs, thrilled by her presence among them. Basil jumps on her.

"My hotshot dog," says Libby, scratching behind his neck. "I like this dog." To Basil, "You're just a pet in disguise."

Libby has a litter of nine dogs named for fish — Grayling, Mudshark, Sockeye. She has another group of six named for pro basketball players — Kareem, Magic, Isiah.

"I don't know if all other dog mushers do this," says Libby, "but I do, 'If this person was a sled dog, who would they be?'"

Before the 1989 Iditarod began, Libby knew she'd be carrying the weight of her own hopes and the expectations of thousands of fans on the back of her sled. Former champions maintain a special status, and once a musher has won the big race once, they forever seem to loom as a threat to do it again.

Still, Libby was no favorite that time. Too much time had passed. The fans, the mushers, knew that if there was a woman to watch, it was Susan Butcher. Butcher herself was watching for men. She was honest enough to admit it.

"Libby is not the competition," Butcher said matter-of-factly. "I'm looking at Rick Swenson and Martin Buser as my toughest obvious competition. And Joe Runyan. Based on last year's Iditarod and other races. We don't know what Libby has to offer."

Libby had this to offer: The best of her dogs. Dogs she considers a damned fine team. She has no patience for anyone who says she can't be as good because she and

Garnie split up. She has bred a new team, a young team, a fast team.

"This is the best bunch of dogs I've ever had," she said before the race, "and the dogs I won with were great dogs."

When Libby and Joe Garnie dissolved their partnership, the winning team was split. In 1988, Garnie finished the Iditarod in fourth place. Asked if Libby could win with her own new dogs, Garnie just laughed.

He said at the time it wouldn't mean anything special racing against her and he predicted he'd beat her.

"I raced her before we were partners," Garnie said. "No problem."

Going into the race, Libby knew she was a dark horse.

"In ways, I feel similar to the 1985 race," she said. "In a way I'm out of the picture."

She turned out to be even more out of the picture than she thought. Garnie, too.

The 1989 race was a bad year for both of them. Perhaps something had gone out of the team. Perhaps the dissolution of the partnership did truly mean the end of a first-class team that could challenge for first place.

Ironically, Garnie and Riddles raced each other home to the finish from Safety, 22 miles from the end, and down Front Street to the finish line. But they weren't battling for first and second. They finished 15th and 16th, 76 seconds apart.

Libby was sick much of that race with the flu, and mostly out of sorts. And at the end of the race, her dogs had similar woes. She had to drop four animals in Safety and came in to Nome with only six dogs in harness, one over the minimum.

"I was just fed up," said Riddles.

There was no way Libby could have predicted 1990 would be worse. She had no season at all, not through any fault of the dogs. This time her own body let her down. She needed some repairs.

But if possible, the fame of Libby Riddles spread even wider without her racing at all. She authored a children's book based on the exploits of good old Danger that arrogant cat. *Danger the Dogyard Cat* was an immediate hit. And Libby started getting different kinds of endorsements. She became the spokeswoman for United Building Supply of Anchorage. A woman as tough as nails selling nails.

One of the pictures of Libby as part of the advertising campaign has her wearing a hard hat.

That's certainly another kind of view of the first woman to ever win the Iditarod. But one picture will always remain clear in the mind of Libby Riddles.

"Every time I get in the jet and fly over it all from Anchorage to Nome," says Libby, "I think, 'Me and my dogs—we've gone all that way.'"

DeeDee Jonrowe
of Willow

Top Dog Soon?

DeeDee Jonrowe walked door to door between the little wooden boxes in her backyard in Willow, listing to one side as she hauled a heavy plastic bucket.

At each of the 62 little houses—too big for dollhouses, too small for people houses—she stopped, put the bucket down, and scooped out a dish full of steaming glop.

"Eat it kids, it's good for you," she cooed.

The kids barked in response. Most of her sleek, athletic, husky racing dogs lapped greedily at their dishes. Jonrowe, wearing a thick, green snowmobile suit, and peeking out from a blue knit hat, grinned.

"They like liver a lot," she said. "I would say better than other kids."

Not all of them. Some were picky eaters. Some were sloppy eaters.

"Anzak, he'll spill it if you don't watch him," said Jonrowe. "You've got to stand over him."

Jonrowe stood over him and the dog slurped neatly.

The sun reflected brilliantly through the trees on a minus-9-degree afternoon. Just feet away, heading directly out of the 6-acre yard behind the large cedar home, that is tucked off the highway about 75 miles north of Anchorage, the trail led to Yentna, to Skwentna, and beyond.

"I can go to Nome from right here," said Jonrowe.

Funny thing, that's where the Iditarod goes. Is this a shortcut?

Jonrowe laughed. "Maybe."

Maybe the shortcut to Nome runs through Minnesota. Jonrowe has been crowned the queen of Minnesota. In January, 1989, she won her first major sled-dog race, dominating the field to win the 500-mile John Beargrease Sled Dog Marathon from Duluth to Grand Portage and back.

And she did it in grand style, too, shaving 5 hours, 40 minutes off the course record. Jonrowe won in 97 hours, 25 minutes, 49 seconds and stamped herself as a contender in the 1989 Iditarod Trail Sled Dog Race from Anchorage to Nome, the race she really wants to win.

You could hear the echo of male mushers groaning. "Oh no, not another woman." A man hadn't won the most prestigious of long-distance sled-dog races since 1984. Libby Riddles became the first woman to win the race in 1985 and Susan Butcher owned the title the next three years. Joe Runyan of Nenana stopped the female streak later in 1989.

Winning the Beargrease didn't mean Jonrowe can win a race twice as long over terrain twice as tough, but coupled with her ninth place 1988 Iditarod finish, it was an indicator that she was a threat. Clearly, Jonrowe was coming on and the men who bristle at the sight of joke T-shirts that read "Alaska: Where Men Are Men and Women Win the Iditarod," were taking her seriously.

"I think that there are eight or probably 10 top contenders that I would be worried about," said Jerry Austin of St. Michael prior to the 1989 race. Austin is a friend of Jonrowe's who has six top-10 Iditarod finishes and is regarded as one of the wise men of the trail. "And I'd put DeeDee in there."

Austin was proven correct. Right from the beginning of the 1989 race, Jonrowe was with the frontrunners. Everyone should have suspected Jonrowe would be a contender after ABC-TV made her an auxiliary member of its coverage team by strapping a $1^{1}/_{2}$-pound minicamcorder to her sled to show the world a somewhat shaky view of the terrain mushers cover.

Jonrowe was loose and relaxed and she chuckled about her TV role.

"They'll get an hour and a half of the wheel dog," she said. She imitated an announcer: "Here's the wheel dog going to the bathroom."

The Iditarod is usually a race of attrition and although Jonrowe was racing strongly and she had positioned herself in the top five when the leaders turned for the Bering Sea coast in the village of Unalakleet, there was one foreboding sign that would lead close observers to understand that Jonrowe no longer thought she could win.

She arrived in Unalakleet carrying her favorite lead dog, Johnnie, in her sled basket, and wearing a frown on her face. One of the dog's paws was hurting and he wouldn't last much longer in the race.

In a moment of weakness, Jonrowe said, "I'm not going to win the race."

Then she backtracked and said the race would be an exceptional challenge if Johnnie couldn't continue. Johnnie tried—until the next checkpoint—but that was it.

Without Johnnie, Jonrowe resorted to using inexperienced leaders over the final 270 miles of the race. Those leaders came through and were on the verge of bringing her into the finish in Nome in third place when they rebelled.

The team was about four miles outside of town where spectators begin to congregate and line the trail to cheer the mushers home.

"You could just see town," said Jonrowe. "It was awful."

What was awful was this: the dogs became confused by the sight of so many people and refused to run anymore. They thought they were at a checkpoint at least and deserved food, water, and rest.

"It was the domino effect," said Jonrowe. "Of course, there's nothing you can do about it."

When the leaders lay down, the other dogs lay down. Jonrowe frantically tried to coax them to run. But after 10 minutes she realized it was useless. The dogs had called for their own coffee break and they were going to take the break. It was about 3 o'clock in the afternoon and the sun was strong overhead. The dogs were probably imagining they were at the beach.

"My first reaction was that my heart kind of went into my stomach," said Jonrowe. "There was no getting them up."

The crowd dispersed and Jonrowe hoped that would convince the dogs it was time to roll on. She tried to get them running after a four-hour rest and they wouldn't budge then either.

Finally, at about 8 o'clock, the dogs decided it must be time to run again, though once they hit the final stretch approaching Front Street, they seemed to be spooked by the crowds again and Jonrowe had to walk in front of the team.

The delay cost Jonrowe one place in the standings — she finished fourth — and $7,500 in prize money. She was not thrilled about that, but she was more upset at the suggestions from people that her dogs let her down. That overlooks that the dogs and musher are always a partnership and must work as a team at all times.

"I don't feel like those dogs let me down," said Jonrowe. "Yeah, I was disappointed, but not in the dogs; in my ability to foresee the situation and prevent it. Stuff happens and you learn from it. You go from there."

Even if the Iditarod finish was tinged with disappointment, it did nothing to dispel the idea that 1989 was Jonrowe's breakthrough year. Minnesota set the tone.

Jonrowe did not go to Minnesota to see the 10,000 lakes. She went to win $10,000 — first place money.

"I felt like we could be a top finishing team," said Jonrowe. "And I also went into the race thinking we could win the race."

That she succeeded is testimony to her growth as a musher, her increasing confidence, and a belief that her dog yard has the depth to produce both Beargrease and Iditarod teams in the same mushing season.

The Beargrease began at night in downtown Duluth and the country-bred Alaska dogs were a little frightened by 10 road crossings in the first 10 miles and the rows of cheering people. Then Jonrowe's headlamp quit approaching the second checkpoint, 47 miles into the race. The dogs went straight in the dark instead of turning; that cost her 20 minutes.

"I was a little mad," she said, "but I was thinking, 'Just shake it off.' By the fourth checkpoint, 130 miles into the race, I was first. At that point, I felt like if I didn't do anything stupid, the dogs could win the race."

Unlike most other races, handlers are permitted on the course during the Beargrease and Mike, Jonrowe's husband, was able to help.

"I turned to him and said, 'This is our race to win,' " said Jonrowe.

Mike saw another 370 miles of racing ahead.

"I'm not one to count my chickens," said Mike later. "I had a healthy respect for the other mushers."

DeeDee's instinct was correct, though. Once she had the lead, she lengthened it. It was a special moment when Jonrowe's dogs trotted across the finish line in Duluth, the payoff for 10 years of labor and thousands of miles of mushing.

She was a winner at last.

DeeDee Jonrowe developed a love of animals as a little girl. She was given a pet dachshund when she was only six weeks old, but she couldn't keep animals very long. She was an Army kid, born in West Germany, living in Greece, Ethiopia, and Okinowa.

But when the family moved to Round Hill in Northern Virginia, where she attended high school, Jonrowe was able to keep two horses in the backyard and 35 guinea pigs in the basement.

Even in college, at the University of Alaska Fairbanks, where she majored in biology, Jonrowe used to bring stray dogs home to the dorm.

"My roommate would get kind of mad," said Jonrowe.

Jonrowe laughs at herself as she tells this story. It seems there's still something of the little girl about her, perhaps emphasized because she's only 5-foot-2. She has an appealing, upbeat manner, light brown hair with a hint of red that touches her shoulders, and a radiant smile that disarms people and makes her look younger than her years.

Sometimes she sounds pleased just to have a real home. "I never had a washer and dryer before," she said.

Jonrowe's parents, Ken and Peggy Stout, stressed being well-rounded. Sound mind, sound body. Jonrowe took gymnastics, ballet and tap-dancing lessons and played basketball in high school and at UAF. But she craved something more. Being well-rounded sounded good, but just being OK wasn't enough. She wanted to be great.

"I wished I was excellent at something," said Jonrowe. "That was my frustration. I wanted to excel. I was pretty good at a lot of things. I wished I could have been one of those child Olympians."

She wasn't. And she wasn't a mushing prodigy, either. DeeDee met Mike Jonrowe while they were living in Bethel in interior Alaska, and both working for the state Department of Fish and Game. DeeDee, who also fishes commercially, enjoyed her job but found that the bright lights of night life in Bethel consisted of the Northern Lights and little else.

So in 1979 she bought a five-dog team and started mushing for entertainment. The next winter she raced in the Kuskokwim 300, the big local race and a key Iditarod prep. Often, the biggest problem mushers face in that event is fearsome weather.

In Jonrowe's first Kusko, a howling wind drove the chill factor to 90 below zero.

"I wasn't prepared and the dogs weren't prepared," she said.

Bad things happen to the ill-prepared in the Alaska wild. Jonrowe tied her way-too-much equipment on her sled — she says it looked like the Beverly Hillbillies' truck — the dogs lay down and refused to run and she had to be rescued by snowmachine.

"I was big-time cold," she said.

Jonrowe didn't quit, though; she learned.

A couple of months later, she entered the Iditarod and finished 24th.

"I was real scared the first night," said Jonrowe, "because it was at night I'd had troubles in the Kusko."

Many of the guys—Jerry Austin, Rudy Demoski, Don Honea—were generous with advice, she said.

"I received a lot of strength and encouragement," she said. "They were just wonderful. There were a lot of other people out on the trail who didn't have any time for me."

Austin said it's taken time for Jonrowe to make the right decisions about what to carry on the trail.

"She'd carry three times the amount of dog food she needed to get to the next checkpoint," said Austin, "all the batteries needed for the whole race, and way too many clothes. She's become equipment conscious. It just takes quite a while for people to get the hang of it."

For a while Jonrowe traveled the trail with Sue Firmin, another racer. They ran nearly the entire race together three times. They became close friends and helped each other through rough spots, but they may have slowed each other down, too.

"There's a stage in your career where that's a help, then there's a stage where it's best to be on your own, because you're only as good as your weakest dog," said Jonrowe.

Jonrowe found out just how unforgiving the Iditarod can be. In 1983, she hit a tussock and her sled cracked. She traveled 90 miles across the Farewell Burn area into the village of Nikolai guiding 15 dogs with a death grip on the handle bars. She finished 15th in that race. In 1984 the brakes broke near Finger Lake and she had to drag her feet to slow down. She finished 30th.

Jonrowe knows those things come with the territory, but she was still discouraged. She felt she wasn't improving. She wondered if mushing was going to be one more thing she wasn't great at. She skipped the 1985 race, but was sixth in the Kuskokwim 300 that year, her first top-10 finish in a major race.

It took until 1988, though, for Jonrowe to move up to the next level. She was fifth in the Kusko and had her ninth in the Iditarod. It was coming, but slowly. She was breeding her own dogs, building a kennel, and buying and leasing dogs from Susan Butcher. Butcher, the perennial winner of the Iditarod, had become a friend.

There is a vision of Butcher as a driven competitor, but Jonrowe said Butcher has always offered advice liberally and has helped make her into a better musher, even if that means she's now a top challenger to Butcher.

"I'm incredibly appreciative of it," said Jonrowe.

Butcher said she sees something of herself in Jonrowe — her dedication, her deep commitment to caring for the dogs.

"I would rather give her dogs than anybody else because she treats them the way I treat them," said Butcher. "She puts in a lot of time and that's what I do. And she's done it on her own.

"What she can give to me is a good mushing friend. The more you win the more people stay away and don't share. It's fun to have friends who do the same thing."

Bob Sept, a veterinarian who runs the Bering Sea Animal Clinic in Anchorage, has known Jonrowe for years. He knew her in Bethel and is a past chief Iditarod veterinarian. Jonrowe, who also has raised champion show cats, has gradually developed the expertise in caring for her dogs as athletes, he said.

"It involves a lot of time," said Sept. "You just can't glance at them. You've got to pick up their paws, look in their mouths.

"She has the real desire to win now. In order to be competitive you have to do things right over a period of years. This thing has not come overnight."

Indeed. It took 10 years to get win No. 1. Beargrease. Ten years and so many thousands of dollars that Jonrowe is scared to count.

"It was a long time coming," said Jonrowe. "It's worth every dime."

Winning the Beargrease and finishing fourth in the 1989 Iditarod changed Jonrowe's status. In the game of Iditarod poker she now brings more chips to the table than ever before. She's a player. That showed in 1990. There was little doubt for that race that Jonrowe was high on the list when contenders were mentioned.

The Alaskan Interior saw record snows in the winter of 1990 and no one knew what to expect when the race began in Anchorage in early March. Would there be more snow? Would that slow down the dogs for the first since 1985? Would storms interfere and pin down teams in tent city camps? It seemed possible.

In the early going, just north of Anchorage, the mushers were soaked by rainfall. Rain? Then whiteout conditions followed in Rohn. For a while things seemed to be moving at a crawl. And there was so much snow piled beside the trail that any stop not right at a checkpoint was turned into a major operation.

"I was using snowshoes just to feed my dogs," said Jonrowe. "Everything you did took that much more energy because you were wallowing in snow."

But then the weather began cooperating and the mushers began moving swiftly again. Soon they were up to the usual pace, headed for Nome at a rate that put them on Front Street in 11 days and change. Same kind of time Butcher and Runyan had run since 1986.

Jonrowe was again in the hunt until the final miles, but once again her worst experience of the race came close to the finish. This time the incident which cost her occurred in White Mountain, 87 miles from the end.

When she arrived at the checkpoint, two stops from Nome, again in fourth place, the bag containing her dog food and supplies was missing. A wild search produced nothing but wasted time. The bag did not turn up until after she had mushed out onto the trail.

Then, in the run between White Mountain and Safety, 22 miles from the end, the batteries in her headlamp went out. She could easily have been lost in the darkness, but musher Tim Osmar of Clam Gulch played good samaritan and allowed her to follow him into town as long as she didn't pass him. So Jonrowe finished fifth.

"It cost me a position and $5,000," said Jonrowe of the missing bag. "How come I have to have theatrical endings?"

The next time Jonrowe has a theatrical ending in the Iditarod, she hopes it's because she's the winner.

"The year's coming," said Jonrowe. "We're going to win the race."

Jonrowe was ready to win a race when she took the Beargrease. People expected it. But even then she had six leased dogs in her team. In 1990 she had only one. In the future, every dog in the team will be a Jonrowe-bred dog, part of her expanding 110-dog kennel.

Jonrowe has the dogs now, dogs with heart and experience, and she's got the experience herself. She believes she can win the big race.

The little girl who so desperately wanted to be great at something may have found it.

Joe Redington
of Knik

Born to Run Dogs and Races

The Father of the Iditarod became the father of his first husky only 15 minutes after arriving in Alaska.

Joe Redington, Sr., and his family crossed the border from the Yukon Territory of Canada that day over 40 years ago and looked at the gas gauge. While Joe filled up the tank, his wife Vi petted a puppy in need of a home.

The Redingtons had come to Alaska with $18, looking to homestead and mush dogs. Dodger was the first. He wasn't lonely for long.

"By the second year, we had 50 dogs," said Redington.

Today, as you walk amid the trees on Joe Redington's land in the Matanuska-Susitna Borough community of Knik 60 miles north of Anchorage, crunching snow with your footsteps, you walk among 300 to 500 barking, yapping thoroughbred animals who were born to run. These are Iditarod animals. They run for the 73-year-old patriarch and famed cofounder of the "Last Great Race on Earth."

Long-distance sled-dog racing is a different world now than it was in 1948 when Redington bought five racing dogs for $35. Now a Redington-raised lead dog might cost $2,500 and a well-bred racing dog might cost $1,000. To run the Iditarod with a leased team will cost a musher $25,000.

It's different in large part because of Joe Redington, and the Iditarod is what it is today in large part because of Joe Redington. He is a breeder and a racer, one of the best mushers in the world. But more important than any of that, he's a founder.

There have now been 18 races over the frozen, snow-drifted miles from Anchorage to Nome, with prizes that have reached as high as $50,000 for first place and total purses of $250,000. Nationwide television exposure is now expected.

So it may be difficult to recall that the Iditarod did not explode upon Alaska full blown and full grown.

In the beginning it took more than fast dogs and stout hearts to run 1,100-plus miles across the Interior. It took faith and sweat. They were supplied in abundance by Redington.

By the mid-1960s Redington was lamenting the lost tradition of sled dogs running long distances and he thought it was a shame that the old Iditarod trail, used for mail delivery and the famous diphtheria serum run to Nome in the 1920s, didn't have its historical significance noted. At the time, the only dog races were sprints and in the villages throughout rural Alaska snowmachine power was replacing dog power.

"I knew something had to be done to save the dogs," said Redington.

Redington, the late Dorothy Page, and others in the Knik-Wasilla area decided in 1967 to organize a race on the trail. Even then Redington said he pushed for the idea of a 1,000-mile run from Knik to Iditarod and back.

"No one took me real serious," he said.

But they did get a two-day sprint race going on the trail in honor of the serum run and musher Leonhard Seppala, who had died shortly before. The race came off as part of the celebration of the hundredth anniversary of Alaska's purchase from Russia. It was a big success; but when it was over, there was also a big debt.

Redington had put up his land in Knik as collateral and almost lost it. Bill Egan, then governor, rescued him, he said. It would have been easy to get discouraged, but Redington never quit on the concept of dogs racing across Alaska. Maybe the end of the race trail was simply in the wrong place. After all, Iditarod was a ghost town, far removed from the glory of its mining heyday.

"People asked, 'Where the hell is Iditarod?' " he recalled. "So I said, 'Okay, you've heard of Nome?' That got people's attention."

Redington had been a paratrooper during World War II and worked for the Air Force using dogs to go into the bush where helicopters could not. So he turned to military friends for help in recharting the trail that had been idle for decades. Lots of people said he was nuts, but others were intrigued by the idea and volunteered to help raise money.

"We just kept at it," said Redington.

Redington relishes talking about the old days, when nothing was for certain. He recounted his view of the start-up of the Iditarod and his observations from the trail in a booklet written with Marilyn Carter in 1990 entitled *Iditarod Trail: The Old and the New*. In it, Redington states,

"I didn't even know at the time what kind of trail there would be to use, as it hadn't been in service in 40 years."

There was no race in 1968 but there was another sprint race in 1969, 28 miles long. Quite a difference from the many-days event contemplated by Redington.

By 1973, there was a real distance race. The first Iditarod. Thirty-four mushers, some of them reluctant, some of them excited, set out for Nome and the chance to win a piece of the $50,000 prize. George Attla, Herbie Nayokpuk, and winner Dick Wilmarth were among the more famous entries. Joe Redington was not. His dogs were, though. Son Raymie was racing them because Joe was back in Anchorage still trying to make sure there was a genuine purse to pay out the prize money.

What was that first endurance journey on the trail like? Different, for sure, in intensity to what it became later.

"I thought it was all right," is the way Raymie remembers that new-fangled racing. "It was something different. No one was in a big hurry. Everybody camped together."

Joe Garnie, a top Iditarod musher from Teller, is one of many who gives Redington credit for reviving long-distance mushing.

"He brought dogs back alive in Alaska," said Garnie.

Redington has plenty of gray hair now, and he probably got his first strands of it organizing that race. When the first musher reached Nome, the purse was still $3,000 short. Redington persuaded a friend to make a loan.

Humble beginnings, all right. But since then the Iditarod has thrived, and Redington has thrived with it. Redington has raced 16 times and finished as high as fifth on four occasions. In 1988, he led a good chunk of the race.

Redington runs a musher-training school and raises huge numbers of dogs, which are so respected in quality that top mushers and newcomers borrow them. He has more friends than he has dogs. Even the best have learned from him, notably Susan Butcher, the four-time champion who pitched a tent on Redington's property and trained with him several years back.

"Joe is an absolutely phenomenal guy," said Butcher, who said she learned a lot from both him and Vi.

"He's what I call a real Alaskan. I think he taught me what it is to be a real Alaskan and how to deal with life in this frontier. I was a good outdoorsman, but he taught me that no matter how bad a situation he gets himself into, he thinks, 'Well, I'll get out of this one.' It's patience."

Garnie once leased a team from Redington and spent two months training at his camp with him.

"I can tell you, being in his training camp was a real treat," said Garnie. "I learned a lot working with him."

Redington is a bit hard of hearing these days and has more wrinkles in his cheeks than he had when he first came to Alaska. He has good reason to feel proud of what the Iditarod has become, with its nationwide TV coverage, reporters converging in the state from Outside, and the familiarity that coverage has brought. But he still doesn't quite believe it.

"I never realized it would get that big," he said. "I knew it was good, but I never knew it would be worldwide. There isn't a week that goes by that I don't get a call from France, Italy, or West Germany."

Would-be mushers from all over the world want to talk to the Father, the man who started it all, the man who can teach them how to challenge themselves, and the man who also has the dogs necessary for rent.

Redington has seen the trail become part of the national trail system, seen the race on national television, seen pupils race and finish the Iditarod, and seen a couple of sons race to Nome, too.

It has been some journey for the man from Bucks County, Pennsylvania, who was lured north by Jack London's tales, the man who thought he might use English sheep dogs for mushing, the man who has mushed over 150,000 miles in four decades. What's left to accomplish?

Oh yes, there is one thing. Joe Redington, born in 1917 and with a birthday just a month shy of the race each winter, wants to win himself an Iditarod title. He jokes that he would have won it in 1988, when he led for five days, but he really had the best interests of this supposedly toughest of all races at heart. "It wouldn't have looked good," he said, "if a woman won it and then an old man." He paused. "But I'm going out there and try to win it."

A bold goal for a septuagenarian. Can he do it?

Bob Sept, former chief veterinarian and former president of the Iditarod Trail Committee, said he thinks Redington remains a dangerous competitor, is perhaps even more of one than he was in the early days.

"I don't think he had the competitive fire he has now," said Sept. "All along people have thought he had the dogs to win this. In terms of technical ability, it's there. The question is the fatigue factor. He's tougher than a boot. I'd hate to say he couldn't do it, 'cause he could."

Redington finished ninth in the 1989 race, still high in the money. His share was $9,000. It was also Redington's fastest time for the distance. He reached Nome in 12 days, 2 hours, 57 minutes and 16 seconds.

Training for the 1990 race went well. Redington finished third in the Copper Basin 300, one of the shorter preps for the Iditarod, but was surprised by the intense cold he faced. The temperatures held steady at 30 to 50 below zero.

"I wasn't used to that cold," said Redington.

Since one would expect Redington would have seen just about everything, that proves the Alaskan Interior and sled dog racing conditions are always changing. In fact, during the 1989 race, as Redington mushed into the Bering Sea coast town of Unalakleet, the night sky was tinted with a shimmering glow of red. The sky wiggled and the darkness turned bright. It was the Northern Lights, out of control, brilliant, leaving men open-mouthed at their glory.

As weary as Redington was from a long day on the trail, he couldn't tear his eyes away from the sight. A few hours earlier, as he crossed the Yukon River, he almost ignored the trail for the lights above so spellbinding were they.

"They were the best Northern Lights I've ever seen," he said. There is always something to remember from every race.

Redington's 1990 race, however, went poorly from the start. For some reason his dogs didn't want to eat and Redington foundered around 50th place for many miles. Then the dogs revved up and Redington began passing mushers. He passed a bunch, but ran out of trail. His 27th place didn't look good on paper.

Another musher may have taken the low finish as a sign it was time to quit. Another musher may have taken 27th place as an indicator that the bones were getting old. Redington looked at it another way: the dogs rebounded and came in strong. To him, that was the proof he needed that he can still be in the hunt.

"I'll keep doing it as long as I'm competitive," said Redington.

And he still feels that he is competitive.

One reason for that is a recent change in training methods. Until a few years ago, the top contenders didn't run their dogs before snow covered the ground. Then they started developing summer training programs. Redington didn't adopt that tactic at first, but now he has, with his favorite, Luna, in lead.

"I've never been real serious," said Redington. "I've got a point to prove. I think I can do it."

Norman Vaughan
of Trapper Creek

"Get a goal and stick with it"

When he drives along the highway, people honk at the "Norm to Nome" message on the back of his truck. When they approach him on the street, they ask, "Are you going again?"

Yes, Norman Vaughan is going again. He is the youngest 84-year-old in America and he will point his dog sled out of Anchorage to Nome, some 1,100 miles away, for as long as he is able, for as long as he still draws a breath.

"People say, 'There's that old guy again this year. He ought to know better,' " Vaughan said. "They ask how old I am. I say 'Eighty-four, and someday I'll be old enough to know better.' "

That day hasn't come. It probably never will.

Vaughan is from Massachusetts, but he has lived in Alaska since 1975, when he moved to the state with a dog team and $100 in his pocket.

He has spent a lifetime in the world's coldest places, the Arctic and Antarctic. Norman knows cold. Norman knows wilderness.

"My fascination with the North began because of my fascination with sled dogs," said Vaughan, who has a trailer in Trapper Creek about 100 miles north of Anchorage. "It was almost a reaction against the tropics. I don't enjoy hot weather."

So why shouldn't Vaughan keep going on the Iditarod? He has raced it 12 times. Of course, he's going.

When you pass a certain age, conventional wisdom says you should retire. Time to watch the world pass by instead of being caught up in the whirlwind. Time to give up the action, the life that has sustained you. Time to relax.

Bunk. There is no right time for someone else to tell you to retire. Body clocks keep their own rhythms, keep their own time. Kareem Abdul-Jabbar could play in the National Basketball Association until he was past 40. Hoyt Wilhelm could float knuckleballs until he was almost 50. And George Blanda could kick footballs until he was over 50. Many times they were told to forget it; many times they told others to mind their own business.

Vaughan has heard people say that he should quit, that he doesn't belong on the same snow-covered trail as the Joe Runyans and Susan Butchers, champions racing for the glory and the money.

The Iditarod Trail Sled Dog Race may be a championship race, but it has always been and most fans believe always should remain a hybrid race, with room for those chasing excellence in the front and those chasing the experience in the rear. At the back of the pack, Vaughan doesn't interfere with the racers.

Hardly a day passes in sports without the speculation that so-and-so's era has passed. Time to make way for youth, the argument goes.

But, really, why shouldn't a baseball star hang on to the spotlight one more year if he can? He is doing the thing he loves best, and all he might have to look forward to is 25 years of selling insurance.

Yes, there is a difference between running the Iditarod through life-threatening blizzards in the middle of nowhere and spring training in Arizona. There's a life-and-death difference. In one race Vaughan came close to suffering frostbite before being aided by a television reporter; in another race he had to be airlifted off the trail after breaking six ribs and being stranded for 30 hours.

But it is hard to refute Vaughan's argument that he is probably safer in the race, with its manned checkpoints along the trail, than he is when he goes out for a lonely training run from his Trapper Creek home.

In fact, record snows during the winter of 1989–90 meant that mushers training in the Matanuska-Susitna Valley north of Anchorage ran serious risks of moose attacks. The deep snow meant the moose were desperate for food and were more likely to be encountered on cleared trails. A moose assaulted Vaughan's team during a training run, maiming three dogs and knocking them out of the Iditarod.

Vaughan, who has a firm handshake, white hair, and a slightly stooped walk, seems more vigorous than frail, and he speaks energetically.

"Nobody makes me run the Iditarod," said Vaughan. "I want to run it. It's a challenge of your own endurance and your devotion to your own sport. There should be no age limit to that."

His ruddy face is easily recognizable sitting in a downtown Anchorage restaurant eating lunch. Several sandwich buyers approached to wish him luck.

What does Vaughan say to those who say he might regret doing the race, that he might die during it?

"You're wrong," is what he says. "And if I should die I'd be doing the very thing I most like to do, which is driving dogs with and among the world's greatest drivers."

Iditarod winners become folk heroes in Alaska. Only a select few have gained that celebrity without victory. Joe Redington, one of the founders of the race, is one who has, and just to show that age is no impediment to success, he remains a top-10 racer in his 70s.

"I think there should be a place for everybody," said DeeDee Jonrowe of Willow, who raced in the Iditarod for years before becoming a top-five finisher. "I felt really strongly about that in the years when I was struggling in the middle of the pack.

"I really think Norman's an inspiration. You should see all the senior citizens waiting for him in Nome. I think it's wonderful. I love to see people follow what they do as long as they can."

It's not only senior citizens who maintain an interest in Vaughan's progress. He gets mail from elementary school children, too. One school sent 100 letters and one of the kids asked not only for the names of all his dogs, but also for the names of all the dogs in the Iditarod. That's one question he couldn't answer, at least not to a child.

He has an easy answer for an adult with a sense of humor.

"All dogs on the Iditarod are called SOB at one time or another," he likes to say.

A few years ago, the Iditarod Trail Committee adopted a rule aimed at keeping Vaughan out of the race. Mushers were required to reach the finish in Nome within five days of the winner. Vaughan fell farther behind than that and was disqualified. But he ignored the ruling and mushed into Nome anyway.

It costs thousands of dollars to raise and race dogs in the Iditarod and Vaughan has many sponsors, including 10th & M Seafoods in Anchorage, Dow Chemical, and Blondie's Restaurant in Anchorage. He was extremely irked when the follow-the-leader rule was adopted.

"It costs me just as much money to run the race as it did Susan Butcher," he said of the four-time champion.

That rule is dead now, however. Current Trail Committee president Leo Rasmussen helped wiped the rule off the books because he thought it tampered not only with the spirit of the race but also with the spirit of Alaska.

"For some people, Alaska is a second chance, for some it's a last chance," said Rasmussen. "It's a chance to do something of a lifetime. To turn around and cut people off because they can't compete with the champions of the Iditarod is utterly stupid."

One of the things the Iditarod did instead as a safety measure was to pay the entry fee of a musher to act as a backup sweeper, staying behind the last-place racer.

"What would the Iditarod be without Colonel Vaughan?" said Rasmussen. "If you were 84 years old and you wanted to climb Mount McKinley, I hope to God there's somebody around there who'll help you to the top."

Climbing Mount McKinley is not among Vaughan's adventures, but his life has been lived fully, dangerously, and boldly.

He could fill volumes with his remarkable stories — and is in the middle of doing exactly that. A book is due out. He hopes it is the first of at least two. The University of Alaska Anchorage and Harvard University, which he attended but never graduated from, have asked him to donate his papers to their libraries.

"I'm hanging on to them for now," he said.

Vaughan is a sturdy customer, who mushed dogs in the 1932 Winter Olympics, the only time mushing was a full Olympic sport. He would like to live long enough to see the sport reinstated as a medal event. Since it was a demonstration sport in Calgary in 1988, that's possible.

He was also described by *Alaska Magazine* as part P. T. Barnum and part Peter Pan. He is a guy who does well promoting himself and it's easy to make the argument he's never really grown up. In 1977, he talked his way into President Jimmy Carter's inaugural parade — with his dogs.

Vaughan traveled to Antarctica with Admiral Richard Byrd from 1928 to 1930. There's a mountain named for him in Antarctica and he was given a Congressional medal. He was also part of an Army search and rescue team in the Far North during World War II and had the rank of Colonel.

Not only has Vaughan started the Iditarod 12 times, he met his fourth wife, Carolyn Muegge, 37 years his junior, while mushing in the race. At the wedding, Rosemary Phillips, executive director of the Iditarod Trail Committee said, "Colonel Vaughan has proved time and again that he is young at heart, and once again he's coming through."

Over the past several years, Vaughan has been involved in a project to excavate eight U.S. military planes that have been entombed in the ice of Greenland since 1942.

The planes crashlanded and their crews camped in one of the B-17s for nine days until a sled-dog team arrived and led them to the coast. The fliers had been ordered to destroy their "state of the art bombsights." However, a month later it was learned that the bombsight on one of the planes had been missed and Vaughan went back to the site alone by dogsled to get it before it could fall into the hands of the Germans, who had weather stations nearby.

"If I knew I was going back in 40 years I would have put up a good marker," Vaughan said when the expedition began in 1981.

In June of 1990, the search team reached the first plane. Clearly, Vaughan is no couch potato now.

"It's all been consistent with living in the outdoors, traveling by dog team, getting cold once in a while, and getting sweaty once in a while," he said.

People routinely tell Vaughan he has led a remarkable life, but he pshaws that.

"The facts are that I haven't done anything spectacular that anyone else couldn't do, but I've been opportunistic," said Vaughan. "I've had the chances to go some places."

Sure, an 84-year-old is not as sturdy as a 34-year-old. But the Iditarod is about more than winning and losing. It is about fighting the wild to a standstill.

Vaughan has never doubted he could do that. Not then, not now.

"Your every thought and every motion is tempered by thoughts of survival," said Vaughan. "There's nowhere you can let down. If you lose your team, you lose your life. Some days are easy and some days are difficult."

Vaughan showed in the 1990 race he still knows what he's doing. He drove into Nome at dusk on his 21st day on the trail, the 60th of 61 finishers in a record-breaking year for the race.

The previous record was 55 finishers.

Completing the race was great evidence to silence critics, especially since the year before he had to scratch, only 151 miles into the race, with a bum knee.

Vaughan left Fourth Avenue in Anchorage with cheers of "All the way!" ringing in his ears from fans who lined the fence to support him.

"I think that's applicable to senior citizens, middle-aged people, and youth," said Vaughan.

"Get a goal and stick with it."

Vaughan was jubilant at the finish line, joking and laughing with friends and celebrated well into the evening.

On his annual treks to Greenland, Vaughan wears a single set of identification tags. The tags provide his name, the name of the group—the Greenland Expedition Society—and a number, 0001. The U.S. military issues two sets of dog tags, with the second set removed in case of death.

At first, Vaughan joked that his cohorts classified him as already dead. On second thought, he decided something else.

"God made an exception in my case and made me immortal," said Vaughan.

Maybe so, Norman. Maybe so.

2
Old Men and the River

As much as Alaska is a place of cold weather, high mountains and wild terrain, it is as much a place of water. Ocean water is the dividing line for its borders. But river water is where Alaskans have fun.

There is no river in Alaska quite as popular as the Kenai River, a spectacular body of pale green water that is a haven for avid sport fishermen seeking king salmon and red salmon, and for families seeking a pleasant ride in a raft. It is easily accessible to several of the main population centers in the state and sometimes on busy summer days whole new populous cities are created by people who drive their campers and recreational vehicles to the Kenai Peninsula on their weekends or holidays.

Harry Gaines is probably the most famous and colorful fishing guide in Alaska and he has been at his trade for two decades, just about as long as the Kenai has been a popular sport fishery. Gaines has been around a long time and he has seen it all. He's also a fishing guide who makes sure that those who chase the fish have a good time, whether they actually catch any or not.

Gary Galbraith is a generation younger than Gaines, but he's been a man of the river, in quite a different way, for over a decade himself.

Listening to them will convince just about anyone what a special place the Kenai River can be.

Harry Gaines
of Kenai

Smooth-Talkin' Salmon Guide

As the salmon hunters sat down in the boat on the shore of the Kenai River, fishing guide Harry Gaines made them take the oath.

"Raise your right hands and repeat after me," he said.

Four people raised their right hands.

"I solemnly swear I will not jerk my rod when I feel a fish bite," said Gaines.

"I solemnly swear I will not jerk my rod when I feel a fish bite," everyone repeated.

"If I catch a fish I'll tell the whole world who I caught it with," said Gaines. Chuckles all around.

"If I don't catch a fish I won't tell anyone who I fished with."

Everyone laughed. Gaines winked.

Stalking king salmon on the smoothly flowing, green, glacial-melt waters of the Kenai River on the Kenai Peninsula during the short Alaska summer is a sport that attracts thousands of fishermen from all over the world.

But after nearly two decades on the river, 60-year-old Harry Gaines, one-time broadcaster, one-time concert promoter, one-time USO show master of ceremonies, and one-time hypnotist, has learned that leading people to big fish can be equal parts sport, wilderness adventure and show-business. One thing Gaines never overlooks is the show business part.

There are close to 300 licensed guides on the Kenai in southcentral Alaska, but only with Gaines is a visitor from another state or county likely to find himself on the radio. Several times a day the fishing is interrupted to broadcast live reports on where the fish are hiding.

No guide can guarantee a client a fish for the freezer — not even at the $125 a half-day that Gaines charges. But if someone is going to pay that much money for five hours of sitting in a cool river breeze to get skunked, a guide had better make the trouble seem worth it.

Grinning like an elf through a thick, flowing, gray-white beard, the short, chunky Gaines, who resembles Santa Claus with sunglasses, tells fishing yarns and risque jokes as the boat motors up and down a 10-mile stretch of river. The river may run short of fish, but Gaines never runs short of words.

Anything is likely to happen on a Harry Gaines fish report. Sometimes fish are caught and he has to sign off. Last year an enthusiastic angler from Georgia who'd just caught a king larger than his offspring came on the air babbling semicoherently.

The man allowed that he'd been to three county fairs, two hog callings and, ahem, a bizarre sexual event — which he described graphically. But, he said, "I've never seen nothin' like this."

You saw it on the radio.

For once, Gaines was speechless.

The sun's brilliance was glittering diamonds on the surface of the Kenai, one of those rare God-blessed June days when the fat, black clouds were on holiday; plain, old good-to-be-alive weather.

Friends Susan Halleran of Anchorage and Tami Reiser of Nikolaevsk, wanted to make a citizen's arrest of the biggest, fattest king salmon around. Bigger than the 97 $1/4$-pound world record. If they did, Gaines would give them $5,000. That's a standing offer to anyone who catches the record fish with him. Five thousand dollars for a million buck's worth of publicity.

The guided trip was an anniversary present for Reiser, a housewife and mother of two, and a birthday present for Halleran, an artist.

"Here we are, Tam," said Halleran, as she dropped the 30-pound test line of her graphite rod into the water and tilted her face to the sun's soothing races. "Our husbands are working their butts off and we're down here playing."

Halleran wanted to know if the fish had been telephoned, heralding her arrival.

"Did you call them?" she demanded of Gaines. "Did you tell them Susie is here?"

Gaines gave her a hearty "Ho, ho, ho."

But not 15 minutes into the afternoon, still in sight of Gaines's fish camp, it was Reiser who felt a tug on her line. Gaines looked at the rod bending and he got juiced.

"Reel in, you've got a fish," he yelled.

Everyone else spun cranks fast to get other lines out of the way. Two minutes later, Reiser had a fish in a net held by Gaines. He put it in the back of the boat. But it wasn't a giant king salmon; it was a sockeye, a red. An attractive fish, about seven pounds, but definitely not a king.

As it lay in the back of the boat squirming, Gaines bopped it on the head a couple of times with a metal club labeled "Kenai Konkers For Whopping Big Fish." It works.

"If there are reds in there, there's got to be others in there," Gaines proclaimed.

He had lived up to his nickname of "Quarter-Mile Harry," catching fish in sight of his place.

Reiser smiled smugly. Dinner?

"Might be," she said.

Halleran looked at Reiser's dead fish.

Reiser said, "Want me to show you how to do it again?"

A few minutes later, Reiser told the world about her fish—or at least that segment of the world listening to KCSY 1140 AM.

At 1:30 P.M. it was show time on the river. Gaines flicked on a transistor radio. The voice at the other end said, "In a moment, we'll check in with Harry Gaines."

Seconds later, Gaines's voice came from the box. "Thank you very much, and it's a beautiful afternoon out on the Kenai—Right now I'm talking to—" He shoved the microphone in front of Reiser's face. "What's your name?"

Surprised, Reiser blurted her name.

"What'd you catch, Tami?"

"A sockeye salmon," said Reiser.

"We did catch a sockeye as a bonus," said Gaines. "And this is Harry Gaines on the Kenai. We'll be back at 2:30."

It's Alaska Home Companion, with the river as Harry Gaines's stage.

"It's probably the most-listened-to thing in the world down here," said KCSY station manager Buzz Barr. "We get those Anchorage listeners driving in. He's a legend. We call him the legend of the river."

The bites of air time sprinkled between 6:30 A.M. and 8:30 P.M. are scheduled to last 90 seconds each, but you never know.

"We can talk all afternoon, if you want," said Gaines.

No one doubts it for a minute.

Gaines's 1,000 to 1,200 clients a season come from all 50 states and many foreign countries, but Gaines came from somewhere else, too. Waco, Texas, in the beginning, which accounts for the remnants of southern-speak in his voice. But it was a long route through Orlando, Fla; Hobbs, N.M. and through other jobs to the career of fishing guide.

In all of those spots and in all of those jobs, talking a good game earned Gaines a paycheck. He was the master of ceremonies for Air Force special services shows and hypnotized members of the audience. Picked people right out of the crowd, put them to sleep and did David Letterman-type things with them, like stretch their bodies between two chairs and stand on their stomachs. He swears it's true.

Gaines toured the country hypnotizing people on a show featuring Boris Karloff's double as Frankenstein, worked for radio stations in the Air Force and Florida, and went home to Texas to manage a country western band called Jimmy Heep and the Melody Masters.

In 1954, he tried promoting concerts. Booked Elvis Presley into a hall in an Austin, Texas, suburb for $200. Nobody knew Elvis Presley then. Nobody. Nineteen people showed up. Six months later, Presley couldn't walk down the street without girls trying to rip his clothes off.

Gaines promoted Presley again. Sold out four shows, but only made $60. Got jobbed by his partners. So he went back to radio, this time with NBC. He covered the launch of the first unmanned U.S. space satellite in 1958 at Cape

Canaveral and for a while did the Royal Crown Cola portion of the Grand Ole Opry out of Nashville.

They were fun days, said Gaines, but he made little money he and his wife Dorothy were trying to raise two boys.

"I got bored with it," said Gaines of moving around, chasing stories, hustling concert tickets. "It was real dog eat dog and it just wasn't my nature."

He became a cop. For six years, Gaines was a police officer in New Mexico. Then he switched to department store management and in 1968 came to Anchorage to open a Valu-Mart store. It's now Fred Meyer on Northern Lights Boulevard. A couple of years later, he moved the 150 miles to Kenai. His first guiding was taking friends out. It turned into a business — a business he loves.

"Mainly because I meet new people every day," he said. "I get just excited with that person catching a fish as if it was me."

Some of the new faces are celebrities. He's taken Kenny Rogers, Tom Selleck, and former Dallas Cowboys' quarterback Danny White fishing.

Gaines has caught an 82-pound king himself. "It didn't take very long," said Gaines. "It's just like a heavy person. Their maneuverability goes quick."

Maybe he sweet-talked that king into the boat.

As one of his off-season jobs, Gaines operated a barbecue restaurant for a while. Friends got suspicious when he sold the restaurant and introduced "Harry Gaines' Fish Scent" on the market.

"They thought it was the same sauce," said Gaines.

The fish scent is a pink liquid that reminds some people of Pepto Bismol. Gaines sprinkles it on the clusters of tiny, red salmon eggs he carves up and uses for bait. For some reason, the fish were not attracted by the Harry Gaines Fish Scent at the end of Halleran's and Reiser's hooks. Reiser's red was the only fish to commit suicide on one of their lines in a couple of hours of fishing.

Lines were pulled in and Gaines pulled down on the throttle of the 20-foot aluminum hull boat. The boat raced down the river to find a new fishing spot.

The wind was strong enough to part Gaines's beard as he faced into it. Everyone else hunkered down. He parked between Eagle Rock and Beaver Creek.

The channel, the current, the narrowing of the river, all determine the best fishing spots. There were perhaps 15 other boats in the area.

That's not many boats on a perfect day. At the height of the king season, the Kenai can be New York City at rush hour. On July 4 weekend, there might be 500 boats in a 50-mile stretch of river creating their own kind of gridlock.

So many people can be out chasing kings that they catch each other's hooks. It's a very different river people know today from the Kenai of the late 1960s and early 1970s. Then, 15 boats were unheard of.

"It was virgin country," said Gaines.

Dave Nelson, state area biologist for the past 20 years, remembers an empty river.

Guiding was "a very, very rare thing on the Kenai," said Nelson. "People assumed kings could not be caught in glacier water. And the king salmon runs were depressed. There was nothing to catch."

Most anglers caught kings by going to an eddy area, standing on the bank and casting.

"It was long and hard," said Nelson.

Spence DeVito showed them a better way. DeVito, who had been a fishing guide in upstate New York before coming to Alaska, was the first to guide in boats, with Gaines not far behind.

DeVito quit guiding in 1978 and a couple of years ago retired as a Kenai School District official. He laments the explosion of guides and people on the river, but said it couldn't be helped. There's no such thing as keeping good fishing a secret.

"I knew there was no way you could stop it," said DeVito. "When there's fish to be caught, there's no way you can keep people out."

He quit, he said, because he felt like a hypocrite criticizing growth and making money off it. He couldn't watch what was once pristine being destroyed.

"We sold them (tourists) a bill of goods," said DeVito. "They'd go out fishing and say, 'Wow, there's more people than where I live.' I couldn't live with it."

Gary Galbraith, operator of Alaska Rivers Co. in Cooper Landing, some 60 miles away on the Kenai River, specializes in raft trips on the upper portion of the river. He said conditions were horrible by the late 1970s.

"There was noise, wake pollution, congestion, bank erosion and safety problems," he said. "There were these big, huge motorboats. They just drove me crazy. Everybody recognized there was a problem."

In 1984, the Kenai River Special Management Area was created by the legislature. Gaines was appointed to the park advisory board by then-Governor William Sheffield. He had been a member of the Kenai River Task Force that recommended formation of the board to restore order on the river.

The problems were myriad, he said, including "overcrowded conditions, the unruly people, the lack of enforcement, and out-of-state guides leaving people on the beach. It was just running wild in all directions."

New protective regulations were molded. Guides must now fulfill numerous criteria to be licensed and boats can carry no more than 35-horsepower engines.

Walter Ward, district ranger for the special area, praised Gaines for working to preserve the river and to promote professionalism among guides, though Gaines was the only member of the board to vote against the horsepower limit.

"I felt it was unfair not to phase it in over four or five years," said Gaines, "when some people had a $40,000 investment. The 35-horsepower didn't matter, but I thought the state jumped into it too fast."

Gaines said he thinks the changes make it more enjoyable to fish the river than it was five or more years ago. He doesn't think the kings will ever be fished out, no matter how many people fish the river.

"Even if there was another 50,000 people on the river and the kings are migrating through, just a certain number are catchable," said Gaines.

The day's lack of action seemed to support that theory. Few anglers in the area caught anything and Halleran grew anxious.

"It's even gotten to the point where I wouldn't care if you caught a fish, Tami," she said. "It's that desperate."

"Are you talking to the fish?" Gaines admonished.

Just then Halleran had a big hit.

"Come on, Susie's fish!" she screamed as she madly wound the reel.

"Keep reeling. Keep reeling," yelled Gaines as he circled the boat. "Just take it easy. He's a big one. I'll tell you that. Just keep your rod pointed in one direction. He'll keep going in a circle. You're doing good."

Halleran giggled and wound.

When the fish broke the surface, Gaines scooped it into a net and threw it to the floor of the boat. It flopped and bled as Halleran stamped her feet and whooped.

"Wow! I never caught a fish like that," she yelled. "See, that's what they look like Tami."

It looked like what it was—a 27-pound king salmon.

The fish was beaten about the head and gills for a bit with the club and gradually expired. The merriment had just begun, though. Gaines led a fish cheer.

"F-I-S-H," he spelled out. "What's that spell?"

"Fish!" everyone shouted back at him.

"Louder."

"Fish!"

Halleran enjoyed gloating about its sleek silver flanks and impressive size. And sure enough, a little while later she was invited to talk about it on the air. She was not bashful.

"Tell me, what did you do a little while ago?" Gaines asked her.

"I caught a great, big king salmon," Halleran boasted. And then she told the entire Kenai Peninsula that her friend Tami hadn't, "poor thing."

Reiser reached over from behind, grabbed a big piece of leg and pinched.

"Ouch!" screeched Halleran.

"Thank you, Harry Gaines, for another scintillating report from the river, squeals and all," replied disc jockey Dan Donovan.

Dead fish and squeals of delight. That's show business, right?

Harry Gaines, legend of the Kenai River, burst out laughing.

Gary Galbraith
of Cooper Landing

Go with the Flow on the Kenai River

New life. It was everywhere on the river.
On a warm June day on the Kenai River by Cooper Landing, there was new life in the spring air, a hint of sweetness, wilderness fresh air. New life in baby moose nuzzling their protective mothers in the thick trees along the shore. New life in eagles' nests, tucked high in the cottonwood trees. New life in nearly bald ducklings paddling behind mothers.
Most visitors come to the Kenai River to take. They come seeking the king salmon, the big, fighting fish that make their runs through the clear, dazzling green of the glacier-melt waters. They come for the red salmon, and later, for the silvers.

They come thinking of fish and forget the water itself. They ride the river in motor-powered boats chasing the fish. But the river is alive in other ways.

Rarely does the visitor drift with the six-to-eight mile per hour current that passes thick forest, well-spaced homes and campgrounds. This is the river taking you. It is a different view, a more relaxed view.

"The upper river, it's quiet, it's more serene. That's the appeal to me," says Gary Galbraith.

The river is Galbraith's home, his backyard, and he comes across as a gentle man living a gentle way of life despite his powerful build and hardiness as a mountain climber and wilderness man.

"I love where I live," says Galbraith.

Galbraith, 39, operates Alaska Rivers Co. Every day he puts rubber rafts on the Kenai from the yard behind the log home where he lives with his wife Carol and young sons Leon and Jesse, and his dogs, geese, and goat. Actually, the geese have grown up, nurtured by the Galbraiths, and while they do hang out in the river just offshore in view of the house, they're kind of on their own.

Gesturing at the four geese who flap their wings and scoot across a span of water toward him, skidding to a halt next to him, Galbraith says, "Those are mine, but they belong to the river now. I just feed them."

Sometimes Galbraith guides fishermen stalking salmon, but letting the rafts ride the river give him more pleasure.

He has done this since 1978 and he never tires of what the river shows him each day. It is his business, but not in an all-consuming way. He may be the boss, but he is still a river guide, doing the same job his hired hands do. He wouldn't have it any other way. What is the point of living on the river and working in an office? No, the point is to be on the river, experiencing what the river offers.

"I haven't let it grow so I'm not on the river," says Galbraith, who combines his love and his livelihood. "I still get out on the water every day. I love it. Every day it changes for me."

It is an understandable pleasure. On this day the raft "Sweetwater" is making a three-hour, 11-mile trip down the river, from Cooper Landing to Jim's Landing. On other days the trip may last eight hours and wind 18 miles through the Kenai Canyon.

Galbraith is not a pioneer rafting guide. Others sold similar trips more than 30 years ago and others sell them now. Some companies predate Alaska Rivers, but have changed owners. But Galbraith is among the old-timers.

And every day he still sees things that he's never seen before. A few days earlier it was eagles fighting; one must have approached too close to the other's nest.

"Yesterday, we had a moose swim in front of us," he says of a trip he guided. "Actually, he kind of walked."

A moose's feet can touch bottom in most areas of the Kenai.

The green of the Kenai never fails to mesmerize. Only Caribbean islands with white sand bottoms match its color. The Kenai is not a raging river, but not a benign one, either.

The wind affects the current and affects the choppiness of the surface. In this part of the river, no motors are allowed, so the river itself makes most of the noise rafters hear. Often, all that can be heard is silence. As the river turns, the current grows mildly rougher. There are few spots with whitewater, though the curve out of Schooner Bend can splash the raft's interior.

Little islands, little dots of land, appear at wide points. Moose migrate to them to give birth and, in the days after they calve, stay there feeling safe from bears. Harlequins scatter as the raft approaches, but ducks feel confident and unafraid. They don't budge.

After an hour or so, Galbraith, his arms pumping, broad shoulders pulling, turns the raft out of the current to a bank for a picnic snack. Parallel parking.

Cheese, crackers, cold drinks, reindeer sausage, homemade cookies, and fruit are served. A vase with artificial flowers is produced and placed on top of the cooler. All the comforts.

Galbraith grew up in Southern California reading Jack London stories and dreaming of the North Country. He is of average height, with thick dark hair, dancing eyes, a sly smile, and hands rough from working in the outdoors.

Galbraith's demeanor is laid back, but he has done some hard-core climbing. He climbed Mount McKinley, at 20,320 feet North America's highest peak, in 1978 and climbed extensively elsewhere in the Alaska Range, the region in the Alaskan Interior with numerous snow-coated, icy, and dangerous mountains. Among those mountains he scaled are Mooses Tooth and Silverthrone, known in the state as daunting challenges. He's also still an active cross-country skier.

"That's my life, being outdoors," says Galbraith.

Although serious mountaineering seems to be behind him, Galbraith still soaks in the beauty of the heavily wooded area he resides in. Cooper Landing is really just a strip of a few stores and several million trees.

Galbraith is often out among the trees when he's not on the river. The dominating nearby mountain is Mount Cecil Rhode, named for a respected wildlife photographer from the area. Galbraith climbs it one or more times a year.

Galbraith is also an amateur naturalist, which was what his college training was in. He walks rafters from the shore into the woods to examine trees being chewed away by beetles carrying viruses. He calls it his natural history lesson. Every once in a while the picnic attracts a surprise visitor.

"I chased a black bear away with a stick," he says. "If it had been a brown bear I would have run off and left him my lunch. When I got back, the people were all standing in the raft a few feet off shore. They seemed on the verge of abandoning their host, letting him become someone else's lunch.

" 'Hey, come back,' " Galbraith says he yelled.

The raft drifts through the Russian River sanctuary. In a few days, fishermen would be elbow to elbow on the banks, dropping lines. But now the banks are deserted and quiet.

As the raft drifts, more moose play peekaboo through tree branches. Warblers dart low across the water. A beaver's work is noticeable on chewed-up trees, but the beaver stays hidden. Dall sheep can be seen high on the flanks of rugged mountains.

"I see things like that every day," says Galbraith. "I look over and say, 'What's that?' We've had two otters this year. It's such a special place."

An eagle's nest, neatly woven branches forming its sides, is close to shore. The mother's white head pokes above the sides, wary of the passers-by.

On the entire trip, only one fishing boat is seen, and that is off the main channel. On this day, the Kenai is quiet, restful, yet still wild. And very much alive.

You can smell the fragrance of Alaska. It's the sweet smell Gary Galbraith smells all of his working days.

3
Making Friends with the Snow

M any people hate snow. They are intimidated by it. They enjoy pictures of it, but they don't want to drive in it, dislike being out in it.

That's not a good way to feel if you live in Alaska. A person with a phobia about snow should probably move to Hawaii. Snow is a fact of life in Alaska and you can't really hide from it.

Not everyone wants to. Some people thrive in the snow. They have made their peace with it and made the snow work for them.

Bob Baker skis on it — far longer than anyone else. Snow makes him happy. Bill Spencer skis on it, far faster than most other people. They frolic in snow the way some people frolic in the sand.

Shawn Lyons is another guy who has special instincts on snow. For some reason Lyons can adapt to snowshoes better than other people who run and who would seem to be able to go faster. There is a magic affinity between Lyons, his snowshoes, and the snow.

John Faeo works magic, too. He coaxes it out of any snowmachine that he rides, skimming ever so swiftly over the bumps, twists and turns of the wilderness.

Whatever their secret, it seems to work only for them.

Bob
Baker
of Fairbanks

Iditaman: Skiing 210 Miles Takes Grit

Most of a moon peeked out from the clouds on a cold and still night at the West Ridge Ski Trails in Fairbanks. It was minus 11 degrees and the snow was hardpacked, a texture that makes it squeak underfoot. The snow weighing on birch and spruce trees was brittle.

The lighted ski trail is tucked behind the dormitories and classrooms on the University of Alaska Fairbanks campus.

During the day the area is crowded with students, but at night it can be a lonely place.

Every few minutes a solitary figure appeared on the 1.2-kilometer loop. He was heard almost as soon as he was seen. It was the rhythmic sound of a ski being dragged

across the snow, a sound similar to that of a knife blade being sharpened.
Bob Baker in training. Alone in the night and cold when most sane people are curled up by a fire. Knit cap covering the almost military cut of his blond hair, frozen sweat encrusting his thick, blond mustache. Just Baker and his skis.
Baker is the man who owns the Iditaski, the world's longest cross-country ski race, who four times has won the 210-mile race across forbidding territory in forbidding temperatures from Knik to Skwentna and back. It has been Bob Baker's race because it is held in Bob Baker's conditions.
Bob Baker's conditions are tough conditions. Baker is always prepared to ski under any terms. In the night, if he has to. In the cold, if he has to. And alone, because no one can catch him.

B aker, the monster of unpaved, unprotected, wide open ski terrain, really wanted to be a basketball player. But he was 4-foot-11 as a sophomore at Lathrop High in Alaska's second largest city. He showed up for tryouts one day thinking it likely he'd find a spot on the team, then slunk out of the gym without letting the coach know his name.
"I wasn't nearly as good as I thought," said Baker.
Skiing's gain. Baker turned out to be a better skier than basketball player, a better skier than he expected. Especially since he was the only one of eight children of an ex-Air Force couple from nearby North Pole who cared a whit about sports. He's also a successful distance runner and bicycle racer. The rest of the family merely thinks he's different.
As a grownup, in his 30s, Baker is a little bigger than he was at Lathrop, too. He's nearly 5-10 and 180 pounds and

he's developed strength in his thighs and buttocks. Watch him from behind as he skis along the trail. The power is in his kick.

Before he finished high school, had Baker qualified for the Arctic Winter Games in the biathlon, the first of four times he has represented Alaska in that biennial winter sports festival against teams from Canadian provinces. He skied for the university in Fairbanks and twice finished as high as ninth in the U.S. national open championships.

Those accomplishments gave Baker respect in Alaska skiing circles, but winning the Iditaski made him famous. Winning it four times has made him a legend. His name is synonymous with the event, a tough race that takes determination to start, never mind finish or win.

The Iditaski is a challenge of the country and the elements and a certain hardiness of the soul is necessary to push the body so far hauling a heavy sled loaded with provisions, perhaps dodging hypothermia and moose.

It can get to minus-just-about-anything on the Iditaski trail. Most people hide in the house under the blankets when it is like that outside. Not Baker. It will never get colder in the Iditaski than the weather Baker has skied in. No weather is too rough for training in his mind.

"I'd just wait for the coldest nights and go out on the Chena River, north of here, maybe 10 miles," said Baker of the preparation he did for his first Iditaski win in 1984.

The night the temperature dipped to minus 54 at the airport, Baker knew it had to be minus 60 on the river.

"I've nipped my ears," said Baker.

His ears? Baker's lucky he hasn't been found frozen solid, a petrified totem pole of a skier, especially since he doesn't even bundle up much. He wears thin layers and doesn't mess with a ski mask until it's at least 20 below.

"Oh, it bothers me every day I go in it," said Baker. "The hardest part of cold weather is starting in it. Once you get out there and into it, nine times out of 10 you're glad you did."

The tenth time, you do it anyway.

It is Friday evening and almost everyone else has gone home for the weekend from the H&S Warehouse. Baker, a dispatcher for the moving company, remains in his office. He's wearing jeans and a shirt with a patch from North American Van Lines on the sleeve. Usually, he works 8:00 A.M. to 5:00 P.M., then skis for perhaps 90 minutes before heading home. But it's payday and there's extra paperwork to handle.

One driver tells Baker a story about how he was injured in a hockey game. "I pay skiers $4 an hour more," Baker jokes.

Baker has an air of authority about him, but it is less from a commanding presence than from a sense of calmness. He has a sturdy build and, well, a sturdy personality.

"He's very patient," said Sharon, Baker's wife of a decade, who met him when they competed together at UAF. "He listens. When things go wrong it doesn't overpower him. There's something about him. Nothing gets to him."

It is the same way on the trail. Inevitably, in a race as long as the Iditaski, something will go wrong. At some point the body will fail. Then it's up to the mind. You can quit and go to sleep, or you can will yourself to overcome the fatigue and push on.

"If anybody does that race and never feels like quitting, he has a problem," said Baker.

In 1987, Tim Kelley—of Anchorage, a former member of the U.S. Ski Team, emerged as a threat to Baker. It took a record finish of 36 hours, 34 minutes to beat Kelley by seven minutes. That was more than eight hours faster than anyone had gone before. They turned what was anticipated to be a long, slow, slog into a 210-mile sprint.

Kelley says he admires Baker. "He's a class act," said Kelley. "The Iditaski is about the stubbornness to keep going. Someone who is stubborn and doesn't know when to quit—Baker's definitely one of those.

"It's friendly kidding between us. He calls me the old man. I'm a year older. It's a rivalry, but it's also kind of an Anchorage versus Fairbanks rivalry. Nobody from Anchorage has ever won the Iditaski. They like to remind everybody they're the men and we're the yuppie geeks."

No one ever accused Baker of being a yuppie geek. He was sixth in the first Iditaski, won the next two, finished second in 1986, and won in 1987. The race against Kelley was definitely the hardest win. No one ever thought Iditaski racers could go that fast, or that far, without sleep.

"There were a couple of times there we ate with our eyes closed," said Baker.

For much of the 1987 race Kelley and Baker were together, Baker leading.

"I was just like a tour guide for him," said Baker. But Baker slowed between the checkpoints at Yentna Station, 143 miles into the race, and Krota Slough, 159 miles in, and Kelley passed him.

"My grandmother at 90 could have walked past me," said Baker. "It was just a death march."

Kelley powered away and Baker thought he had lost. He was 20 minutes behind coming into Krota Slough. He took no rest there, chased Kelley the eight miles to Big Su, then snuck out of the rest area fast before Kelley could respond.

"I was hoping for 20 minutes," said Baker. "I got eight. That was enough."

All the way into Knik Lake, Baker glanced over his shoulder, watching for a headlamp closing in in the darkness. He never saw one.

Somewhere in the darkness, his body reduced to a two miles per hour trudge, Baker had met himself at his weakest. He was a man drowning who swam to the surface, a man crumbling, whose will became the glue. He came close to falling apart. But, instead, he pulled it together.

"You get to the point of exhaustion," said Baker, "and you tap some emotions, energies, and feelings you cannot play around with in any other event. Physical fitness plays a small role in the winner's circle."

What does a man find when he digs that deeply into his core? Baker can recognize it. He knows he has it. He just can't name it. The word "it" said Baker, is the best he can do. " 'It' sounds real good," he said.

In Baker's first two Iditaski victories, he dominated. But once Kelley appeared, it seemed likely future races would become neck-and-neck battles, too. However, when the 1988 race rolled around, Kelley wasn't there. He had the flu and the Iditaski isn't the kind of race a body wants to be in when it's already been weakened.

They say champions show their best when they are forced to by challengers nearly as good. That would have meant Baker had peaked when he outraced Kelley. But a year later, someone else materialized. John Ferri, a one-time champion who had never gone nearly as fast, suddenly became Baker's shadow.

Prerace discussion focused on strong winds, winds that could rip right through a skier, winds that at the least would make going forward an ordeal.

Baker figured 40 hours was the best he could do for the 210 miles. He was wrong. The winds never mattered to Baker. But Ferri did.

Baker was cruising when, 70 miles from the finish, he became ill. He had to stop, climb into his sleeping bag, and go to sleep. It was not a sound sleep, though, and when Ferri caught him two hours into his nap, the noise woke him.

For a moment, Baker mentally forfeited first place. He felt too weak to race. But then he shook himself, urged himself up, and forced himself to chase the challenger. Thirty miles later, he skied into the Big Su checkpoint one minute behind Ferri. There, he learned Ferri was having foot problems.

Rejuvenated by the chase and the race, Baker cut short his break and skied out with a 15-minute lead. Ferri never caught up again and Baker crushed his year-old course record with a finish time of 32 hours, 50 minutes. Ferri dashed home in 33:52, also far beneath the old record.

"I'm surprised it was that fast," said Baker.

The public Bob Baker is quiet. He isn't chatty, or boastful, but he is proud. Pasted on a door in the kitchen of the 3,000-square-foot house in Fairbanks that Baker built much of, are newspaper stories about his Iditaski exploits.

The log and cedar house is 10 miles north of the university ski trails, in the Goldstream Valley, well back in the woods. Usually, Sharon and the three young children, Gina, Dayva, and Daniel, wait until after 7:00 P.M. to eat dinner with dad after he finishes his ski workout. Suka, the Labrador retriever, and Peter, the parakeet, eat on their own schedule.

It is really a kid's house. Their stuff is tossed around in the living room. Baker's trophies, some very large trophies, are not in a case, not on formal display. They are on shelves, some open to view, some not — much the same as Baker's personality. Some of it is open to view, some not.

"Some people think I'm timid," said Baker. "I think I'm as big a hog as there is. I like the attention."

Some skiers see Baker as a killer on the trails, as a superman who ignores fatigue. They probably don't picture him lying on his back on the rug playing with his infant son.

They would find it harder to picture him on a different trail, making speeches in the Fairbanks area for the Alaska Chapter of the American Lung Association, speaking of the ills of smoking to 3,000 young people.

"The remarkable thing about Bob was how well he related to the students," said former Lung Association Executive Director Deborah Williams. "He was able to put himself in their shoes—

"One thing that's so neat about Bob is that he's such a good athlete but he seems to have everything in great perspective."

You do get that sense about Baker, that he is trying to be the best skier, the best worker, the best husband, the best father that he can be. But maybe the Iditaski is his vice, his indulgence, his bad habit. Everyone has to have one. The Iditaski is the race that identified the thing in him that makes him special.

"Whatever exactly you hate about it is exactly what you love about it," said Baker.

Whatever that something is, that drive or quest to stretch the limits of the body, is in Baker. It convinced him that he must try something even tougher in 1989. There is a long-distance dog mushing race called the Yukon Quest each winter. The race is over 1,000 of mostly empty land between Whitehorse in the Yukon Territory of Canada and Fairbanks. Baker decided to see what it would be like to ski the trail. Fifty miles a day, he figured, would bring him home in 20 days.

If anyone could do that, the sages reasoned, it was Baker. He had conquered all the known worlds on skis; perhaps it was time to challenge the unknown.

Baker made his intention known a few months before the Quest began in February of 1989, but when the race approached, he had the flu. The smart thing would have been to stay home, stay in bed, take two aspirin and drink a quart of orange juice. But once you've touted something, raised expectations, it's hard to back down.

Forty-five miles into the adventure, Baker started throwing up. Disaster. A man burns calories by the million skiing far in the winter. The body will burn out fast without nutrition.

Weakened by his sickness and torn by the perceived humiliation of quitting, Baker agonized as he sat by the side of the trail. He was courting hypothermia, not heroism. One day into the journey, Baker packed it in, decided that reality superseded aspirations. It was not an easy choice to make, even if it was the intelligent one.

"It's going to haunt me for a long time," said Baker. "Some day I will go back out there and do that."

Somehow, you don't doubt that.

On the ski trail behind UAF, Baker paused. He was sweating and his face was as heavily frosted as the tree branches. He glanced up at the sky and smiled.

"A moon," he said.

The moon made him think of the Iditaski. There had never been such a moon for the Iditaski. Maybe the next time the skiers' way would be lit. That would be a perk. No matter, though. Darkness or light, warm weather or cold, Baker would cope. He would be ready for anything.

Baker put his head down and skied away.

Alone.

Bill Spencer
of Indian

Wilderness Games to the Olympic Games

Getting outfitted for uniforms. It's one of the great moments for American athletes at the Olympic Games, the moment they know it's all real, that they belong.

Bill Spencer was excited when he arrived in Calgary, Alberta, for the 15th Winter Games, and he was excited when it was time to pick up his racing duds.

Let's go get that red, white, and blue, right? Wrong. Get your sunglasses ready, instead. When the U.S. Nordic Ski Team hit the Canmore trails, it was decked out in orange and green. Popsicles come in orange and green, not skiers.

"We're pretty conspicuous, there's no doubt about that," said Spencer. "I don't know if they're good looking, but they certainly are distinctive."

Spencer wouldn't care if they hung Christmas ornaments and tinsel on him. He made it to the Olympic Games at age 31 and that was what counted. The guy who grew up on skis in the wilderness of Indian, Alaska, then quit ski racing for six years before coming back, at long last had become an Olympian.

"I've been skiing really well," said Spencer before the Games. "I'm really excited."

It was no surprise that Spencer was dispensing more cheer than Santa Claus before the Olympics. It was no direct flight from Alaska to Calgary for him. It took a lot of time and work, mingled with frustration and heartbreak for him to make it there. There was plenty of reason to wonder if the day would ever arrive.

His older sister Lynn was an Olympic Nordic skier. An older brother, John, was on the U.S. Alpine team. And Bill was a child prodigy on skis.

But he became a burned out teenager who gave up the sport two years after the 1976 U.S. Olympic Trials. He decided to try again in 1983, but his comeback was derailed when he got sick just before the 1984 Trials.

Things started to turn his way in 1987 when he won the 50-kilometer race at the national championships and he had a terrific fall and early winter racing in and around Anchorage.

Then he had the kind of deja vu experience that can give you nightmares for a long time — he got sick just before it was time to race in Minnesota at the Trials.

"I survived the Trials," is the way Spencer put it. "I kind of went into the Trials pretty well rested, but not sharp. I was struggling. I had a little too much volume and I went a little bit flat there. I wasn't on my game at all at the Trials."

Spencer's strength began returning soon afterward. Between the Trials in early January and the Games in February, Spencer grew sharper and sharper. He finished second in a classical style 15-kilometer time trial at the U.S. team's training camp in Utah.

"That was pretty good for me," said Spencer, who had not figured to be a factor at that distance.

There was some of the just-happy-to-be-here outlook in Spencer when he first appeared in Calgary, but he wanted his racing to be something to remember, too. Just because no one thought he or the other Americans had a chance on the trails against the Swedes, the Finns, and the Russians, didn't mean Spencer was content to wave a ski pole at them when they went past.

"I didn't come here just for the Olympics," he said. "I came here to race, too."

It took 12 years for Spencer to be able to make that statement. Even if his uniform colors were orange and green instead of red, white, and blue, Spencer knew that he belonged.

Spencer is a lanky, handsome athlete of 6-foot-1 and about 160 pounds, with boyish good looks. He looks much younger than his age of mid-30s. Perhaps it's because he's spent a lifetime in the outdoors. Doing something outside, away from the city, being hidden in the trees, is the thing Spencer loves.

"I really enjoy the training aspect as much as the racing aspect," said Spencer. "Being in the mountains, running in the woods—it's a good lifestyle. Competing kind of lends legitimacy to my somewhat unorthodox lifestyle."

For quite some time Spencer tried to balance the need to make a living with the need to train full time as a world class athlete. He worried that he was a ski bum with no career and *that*, in part, eventually led him to retire from skiing. Even before the Olympics, that thinking was playing on Spencer's mind.

"Every year it probably becomes a little more acute," he said. "I never really feel like I could get involved in anything that will last for a while because come December I always say, 'See you.' "

It is not as if Spencer is unqualified for a career that doesn't involve skiing on the World Cup circuit. Not at all. He is qualified for so many things it's tough to choose. He has a degree in fish and wildlife management from Montana State, is more than halfway to a degree in civil engineering, has two years of experience as an assistant ski coach at the University of Vermont, and recently began a job as assistant ski coach at the University of Alaska Anchorage.

Beyond that, Spencer is handy with his hands. He has done backbreaking trail work and helped design new trails. He has fixed snowmachines. He has invented a type of roller-ski that is popular with Nordic racers.

And much of that was done after he quit skiing the first time. A hot junior racer, he overdid it and needed a break. The break lasted from 1978 to 1984. He returned to skiing at the age of 28, a time when most other racers are entertaining thoughts of retirement.

"It's an endurance sport in more ways than one," he joked at the time of his comeback.

Spencer regained his spot on the U.S. national team with a little bit of luck. He needed a sixth-place finish in the last qualifying race and barely got it.

"The guy I had to beat broke his ski pole," said Spencer.

Spencer inched his way back into skiing after his first retirement. He was coaching the women's team at Montana State and the sport slowly reeled him in again.

"I needed to do something else," he said, "but I found myself going to races and wishing I could do it again. If I had started back into it and I hadn't made any progress, I would have quit."

Susan Butcher, the four-time champion of the Iditarod Trail Sled Dog Race and the record holder on both the northern and southern routes between Anchorage and Nome, mushes her dog team across the trail just outside of Shaktoolik. The orange ribbon flapping is a trail marker.

(Photo by Jeff Schulz)

Four-time Iditarod champion Susan Butcher congratulates Sonny Russell on his win in the 1990 Kuskokwim 300 in Bethel. Butcher was second. (Photo by David Predeger, courtesy GCI)

Dog musher Libby Riddles, the first woman to win the Iditarod Trail Sled Dog Race, in 1985. (Photo courtesy of United Building Supply)

Dog musher DeeDee Jonrowe of Willow is fast becoming a contender to win the Iditarod. (Photo by Lew Freedman)

DeeDee Jonrowe's dogs grow excited as their master approaches. (Photo by Lew Freedman)

Joe Redington of Knik. (Photo by Lew Freedman)

A playful pup leaps on musher Joe Redington. (Photo by Lew Freedman)

Norman Vaughan, 84, of Trapper Creek.
(Photo Courtesy of 10th & M Seafoods)

Opposite Page:
Norman Vaughan, who has mushed dogs for over 60 years, racing along the Iditarod Trail. (Photo courtesy of 10th & M Seafoods)

Life from the Kenai River on KCSY Radio, it's Harry Gaines. (Photo by Lew Freedman)

Fishing the Kenai River for king salmon with Harry Gaines. (Photo by Lew Freedman)

Opposite Page: Rafting guide Gary Galbraith of Cooper Landing. (Photo by Lew Freedman)

Bob Baker of Fairbanks, the four-time winner of the Iditaski, the world's longest cross-country ski race, is frosty from the trail. (Photo courtesy of Bob Baker)

Opposite Page: Olympic skier Bill Spencer in the 15-kilometer cross-country race during the Winter Olympics of Calgary in 1988. (Photo courtesy of Bill Spencer)

Bob Baker has skis, will travel during the long, dark Alaska winters. (Photo courtesy of Bob Baker)

Iditashoe winner Shawn Lyons explains the lightweight nature of his specially made snowshoes. (Photo by Lew Freedman)

Snowshoe champion Shawn Lyons doing a workout in the woods near an Anchorage High School. (Photo by Lew Freedman)

Opposite Page: A young Art Davidson following the first winter ascent of Mount McKinley. (Photo courtesy of Art Davidson)

Snowmachine racer John Faeo with a few of his many trophies. (Photo by B. J. Faeo)

Legendary Mount McKinley guide Ray Genet. (Photo by Linda Billington)

Opposite Page: Adventurer Harry Johnson in the Los Angeles marathon, one of the 12 he completed in 1989. (Photo courtesy of Harry Johnson)

Top Left: Among Fred Machetanz's most famous paintings are his pictures of polar bears. Shown here is a detail. (Photo by Lew Freedman)

Middle Left: Fred Machetanz of Palmer. (Photo by Lew Freedman)

Bottom Left: Artist Jon Van Zyle at a book signing. (Photo by Lew Freedman)

Below: Alaska wildlife photographer John Pezzenti. (Photo by Lew Freedman)

Top Right: George Attla of North Pole is as fast a sled dog sprinter as they come. (Photo by Lew Freedman)

Bottom Right: Bush pilot Jim Okonek of Talkeetna, a man of many adventures. (Photo by Lew Freedman)

Below: Reggie Joule tries to make it to the other end in the greased pole walk in the World Eskimo Indian Olympics. (Photo by Mark Kelley)

Mount McKinley, the Ruth Glacier, Mount Foraker and other places in the Alaska Range, are the usual Jim Okonek destinations. (Photo by Jim Okonek)

Lynn, Spencer's sister and one of the other children in the family, can understand that perspective. The desire to improve was the driving force in Bill's skiing, she said.

"He has a desire to be the best, to excel at what he does," she said. "His own personal goal is to improve himself."

If Spencer is famous and admired in his home state because he was an Olympic skier, he is probably equally famous and admired because of a race that is not known outside of Alaska at all.

Mount Marathon is a craggy peak in the town of Seward, some 125 miles south of Anchorage. It rises about 3,022 feet above sea level and overlooks picturesque Resurrection Bay. It is impressive and beautiful, and every Fourth of July its treacherous, rocky, dirty slopes turn into an underdeveloped running trail. If you can call crawling nose to the ground in some areas of steepness actually running.

The Mount Marathon race got its start as a bar bet early in the century. It was run for the first time in 1915 and is the second-oldest footrace in the United States, after the Boston Marathon.

For whatever reason — his boldness, his recklessness, his humongous and efficient lungs — Bill Spencer owns this mountain. The race itself is only 3.5 miles, round trip, from the pavement in the center of town to the summit of the mountain and back to the center of town. The only flat parts are on the roads.

Spencer has won the race seven times, including one tie for first, and owns the race record of 43 minutes, 23 seconds, set in 1981 and which has not been approached.

It is an insane race. Those who sacrifice their bodies to the mountain on sunny summer days before spectators numbering in the thousands, who watch through binoculars, often pay a price. They come back to town trailing blood from gashed legs and sometimes needing stitches to fix all the flapping skin.

Yet Spencer loves this race.

"The whole celebration on the Fourth of July in Seward," he said. "There's a lot more going on. The huge background, the tradition behind it. You meet people who come back to it over and over."

That's the atmosphere; but another attraction is the mountain itself.

"The physical challenge is unique," said Spencer. "There is a certain element of hazard in it. You've got to have your wits about you."

People hustle up the mountain as fast as they can and then try to scramble down as best they can without clobbering themselves. In some places, the trail is soft scree. In others, it consists of large, bulging boulders. It's amazing, no one has been killed in the race.

"I think the thing that does it is the soft footing so you can be hell-bent for leather," said Spencer. "Unless you twist your ankle. I'm always a little bit awed by it.

"You're actually coming down to the road in about six minutes. Your ears pop. That is pretty stunning. It's 'Holy smokes.' "

Holy smokes is pretty much the reaction when Spencer runs on Mount Marathon. People consider it evidence that he must be part mountain goat.

The day before his first race in the Olympic Games, Spencer got sick. A cold. Perfect timing. Let's ruin the big moment.

"I've got every cure you've ever heard of," he said the night before the 30-kilometer race.

Spencer never figured to be in a race for the medals — no Americans ever are — but miracles do happen, especially in the Olympic Games. Who would have guessed the U.S. ice hockey team would have won the gold medal in Lake Placid in 1980? Who would have guessed cross-country skier Bill Koch would have been a medalist? But he did it. There was precedent.

"It's a dream," said Spencer of the prospect of winning a medal. "But it's not really attainable. I'd like to be in the top 20 or 25."

How many people can dream dreams of even that magnitude? Not many, including Spencer, as it turned out. He woke up the next morning with a cold and sore throat and didn't race at all.

"I guess I figured that being in this high a caliber of race I might be in the middle of the pack if I was feeling good and I would get beat badly if I wasn't," he said.

Spencer got his chance to race in the 15-kilometer event. It was a sort of Welcome-to-the-Olympics Bill Spencer day. He struggled to a 40th place finish in the 90-man field and then got plucked out of the finish chute for random drug testing. He was the lucky skier chosen, along with the medal winners, to provide a urine sample.

Spencer was so dehydrated that in the hour after the race he force-fed himself cup after cup of water. He drank perhaps 12 cups, or a half gallon, before he was released by the officials.

"You're just so dry, the first eight cups wander off into your system," said Spencer.

The race itself represented reality.

"I came in here thinking that less than 40th would be a disappointment and better than 40th I'd be happy," he said.

Which meant he didn't know quite how to feel in 40th.

Eventually, Spencer also got to race on the 4 x 10-kilometer U.S. relay team and in the 50-kilometer marathon in which Gunde Svan scorched the fastest time ever for the distance.

Spencer was 56th in that race and was suffering with the flu.

"I wasn't sure I'd finish when I started," he said.

But he knew it would probably be his last race ever in an Olympic Games and he wanted to savor the experience. He did know going in that the creeping crud was going to hurt him and prevent him from skiing his best, so instead of wearing that flashy orange and green uniform, he dug an old blue racing suit out of his closet.

"When you know you're going to finish last, you shouldn't wear anything too conspicuous," said Spencer.

In the two years after the 1988 Olympics, Spencer gave up international competition and went after his second college degree in Vermont. When the chance to return to Alaska and coach came up, he took it.

It is his new life in the same old place. Spencer doubts that old place will stir fresh competitive skiing instincts, but that doesn't mean he's going to become a couch potato and get flabby, either.

"I'm going to stay fit till hell freezes over," he said.

And even if big-time skiing is a thing of the past, Mount Marathon still beckons. Spencer's last win came in 1986, but that doesn't mean he's all through with that mountain.

"There've been gaps before," he said, dropping hints about future races.

The big, mean hill that is Mount Marathon will always be there. And Bill Spencer, the master of its slippery slopes, will almost certainly return.

Shawn Lyons
of Anchorage

Cap'n Crunch: Once a year a shoe-in

Alone in the middle of the Alaska wilderness Shawn Lyons shuffled through the frigid night. The snowshoes on his feet broke the enveloping silence. Crunch. One step away from Rabbit Lake. Crunch. One step closer to Skwentna. Crunch.

The competition behind him, the finish line before him, Lyons shuffled into a kaleidoscope. The night became light. The night became a rainbow. Shimmering curtains of celestial light exploded in the sky. The Northern Lights showed the way home.

Lyons smiled and ran. Lyons, with a song reverberating in his head, snowshoed. Snowshoed looking up at the heavens. Snowshoed looking up until his neck just about froze that way. Snowshoed between Knik Lake and Skwentna faster than anyone dreamed.

Just Shawn and the night.

It is 105 miles from Knik to Skwentna. There are no roads in this isolated, frozen region just north of Anchorage that leads to the Alaska Range and Mount McKinley territory. There is mostly deep, drifted snow and a path through a woods more likely to be populated by moose than people. And temperatures that petrify the bones. Minus 40, maybe.

Once a year in early February people strap on snowshoes and see how fast they can go between the two tiny towns. They call the race the Iditashoe. About 10 men and women shuffle off each year to Skwentna. Lyons is always among them. It doesn't take very many steps before Lyons leaves the others behind. He crunches faster, for longer, than anyone else.

The first Iditashoe, in 1985, was two guys just seeing if it could be done. Since then it has been Shawn Lyons's Iditashoe. He won in 1986, then set the record of 27 hours, 8 minutes in 1987. The second-place finisher was 52 miles behind when he finished. And then he won again in 1988. Fresh challengers popped up, but it didn't matter. He won for the fourth time in 1989. And for the fifth time in 1990, even though the race distance was cut short because of awesomely forbidding temperatures. Shawn's shuffle gets him there first.

Five races, five firsts. Not even Lyons would have believed that. After all, he didn't even want to do this dumb race.

"When I first read about it," said Lyons, 'I thought, "They're crazy. I'll never do that.' "

But when he read a call for entries, he thought differently. He'd run some 20 marathons. He'd been hiking in the mountains since his childhood. He loved the wilderness and he knew he could slog forever. One hundred and five miles on snowshoes? Somehow, it shifted in his head from no way to no problem.

"I had no idea what I was getting into," he said.

February, 1986. Lyons was on the Knik Lake starting line, ready to haul his mandatory gear — sleeping bag, stove, food, and the like — to Skwentna. The starter said go and everybody went — running. Lyons was stunned.

"All those guys take off at a run," he said. "And I think, 'We're supposed to run this? A hundred miles? Good-bye.' I knew that some of them would come back to me because I figured you can't run 100 miles, but let's just say the idea of doing well quickly evaporated."

He was wrong. You can't run 100 miles on snowshoes. But you can walk and run four miles an hour. The tortoise kept his own pace and one by one every one of the hares came back to him. When he reached Skwentna, 41 hours, 48 minutes later, Lyons was a winner.

What Lyons didn't know until afterwards was the guys he beat were national champion ultramarathon runners.

"I would have been intimidated," he said. "It would have been like running against Bill Rodgers."

Now Lyons is the Bill Rodgers of long-distance snowshoeing. Ask Bob Baker. Baker is viewed as an iron man for winning four 210-mile Iditaski races, the world's longest cross-country ski race and the Iditashoe's big brother event.

"It's pretty awe-ing to me what he does," said Baker. "I just find snowshoeing a bit of a task, I guess. It's just so slow and cumbersome compared to skiing."

Baker thinks the Iditashoe is harder to do than the Iditaski.

"I think it's harder on your body and everything," said Baker. "It's more jarring. It's just mentally harder. He's amazing."

Lyons is an aw-shucks kind of guy. He's soft-spoken, unprepossessing, and has the build of a guy who's always getting sand kicked in his face in the comics. He has a mop of blondish-brown hair and a beard covering his angular, Abraham Lincoln-type face. He's six feet tall and weighs just 143 pounds.

It may sound giraffe-like, but that, of course, is also the perfect build for the long-distance animal. Long legs, light weight, hardy constitution.

And peace of mind.

Inner peace is important for a man challenging his body in Alaska's winters. The weather can kill. Panic can kill. Whether it is a solo mountain climber, solo skier, or solo snowshoer, a man must be skilled to survive in the wilderness. He must be sure of himself when the wind whips him with icicles and the snow creates a swirling tornado to blind him.

The great Alone does not intimidate Lyons. It is his friend. He crunches across the Iditashoe trail in the dark, often without even a headlamp. The eyes adjust to the night's glow and the vague outline of the trail is enough. Never does he feel the loneliness of the last man on earth in this barren land. Never does he fear the emptiness.

"That's because I've been alone in the middle of nowhere before," said Lyons. "I've never felt nervous. You can be nervous in a huge crowd. Though I spend 90 percent of that race alone, I've never been lonely in it."

When Lyons, now 36, and his five brothers and sisters were growing up in Westwood, Mass., a suburb of Boston, his father Joseph used to pack them in the car and drive to the White Mountains in New Hampshire. Shawn's first trip was as a six-year-old. He climbed Mount Washington, the highest peak in the northeast, before he was 10.

"He had an old army rucksack and he filled it up with cans of Dinty Moore beef stew and off we'd go," said Lyons of his dad.

Lyons's memory retains more of the fondness for the hikes than the stew, but he insists that has nothing to do with his being a vegetarian now.

Lyons said his father, now in his 70s, still runs every day. His older brother Timothy was a star two-miler at the private, Catholic high school they attended and Shawn went out for the track team, too, but didn't last long.

"They got me on the track doing 440s," said Lyons, "and I went, 'Oh, I don't think so.' Not much fun."

Speed kills apparently. So Lyons quit the team, but didn't quit running or hiking. Much later he entered the New York Marathon on three months' training and ran 3 hours, 8 minutes. Going for a long time, he decided, was fun. Between 1976 and 1982, he ran 20 marathons with a best time of 2:45. He recovered from the 26-mile, 385-yard races in a single day, but never got any faster. He still wasn't willing to do 440s.

What Lyons did do was seek out longer hikes and higher elevations. In the summer between his junior and senior years in high school, Lyons hiked the Appalachian Trail, 2,100 miles from Georgia to Maine. Later, after graduating from the University of Massachusetts magna cum laude with a degree in English literature, Lyons spent months climbing and traveling in Nepal, Pakistan, and India. He'd already climbed the trio of Mexican volcanoes that are the third, fifth, and seventh highest mountains in North America. He moved to Anchorage in December, 1984, at least partly because the Chugach Mountains were nearby. They provided an easily accessible playground for climbing and hill running.

As competitive as he admits to being, Lyons said he has pretty much given up foot racing.

"I find more enjoyment being in the mountains," he said. "No matter how exhausted you are, there's always something to enjoy and to take your mind off the discomfort a little bit.

"Sometimes I get criticized for not stopping to smell the roses. But I think that someone who sets out with goals is more in tune with where they are. They're more wide awake most of the time."

There aren't many roses to smell along the snow-covered trail in the Iditashoe, but staying awake is a concern.

Lyons recites poetry to himself and plays classical music in his mind as he goes.

He has built his stamina in recent years by doing speed hikes of more than 24 hours at a time over the 5,000-foot peaks of the near Chugach Range, but the ability to go for a long time has its roots in the White Mountains. There is no underestimating what that youthful background has meant.

"The weather turns a lot worse in the White Mountains than it does in Alaska," said Lyons.

By Alaska standards, the White Mountains, running through New Hampshire and Vermont, are puny. Mount Washington is the highest at over 6,200 feet, but a wind velocity of over 240 miles per hour has been recorded there, so it's not exactly comparable to a stroll around a shopping mall parking lot.

Once, on a three-day, 100-mile hike over peaks in the White Mountains, the snow consistency was ripe for avalanche. Every step was dangerous. The concentration needed there was the same that's needed in the Alaska wild.

"Just keep your wits about you," said Lyons. "That's 90 percent of it. Don't let little things psyche you out or accumulate in your mind as nerve-racking."

Long fingers moved confidently on the neck and strings of the guitar resting across one knee. Wearing dress clothes, Lyons sat on a stiff-backed chair by one wall in the dim restaurant lit only by candles burning on dining tables.

His eyes were shut, closing out all but the notes his guitar sent into the air to mix with the aroma of fresh-cooked food and the atmosphere of intimate conversation.

Snowshoe racing isn't very likely to get on Shawn Lyons's nerves. It is who he is only one day a year. The rest of the days he is Shawn Lyons, musician. If the Iditashoe brings out his intense side, music brings out his gentle side.

Every weekend night, with a glass bowl by his side for tips, Lyons plays classical guitar at the Villa Nova, an intimate Italian restaurant on Anchorage's south side. He has been doing this for about four years. Days he teaches guitar through the University of Alaska Anchorage, and he also writes newspaper classical music reviews. Most of the bookshelves in his home on the fringe of the old Spenard section of the city are filled, not with books but with musical tapes.

Lyons plays few tunes recognizable to the ear trained on American Top 40. His songs have European origins. Some are Spanish, some are English, some are his own compositions. He has recorded an album, though he says many are still left over at home from the pressing of 1,000 copies.

The Villa Nova offers a pleasant environment to play in. It is a cozy place and even when full barely holds 50 people. But still, it is not Carnegie Hall. The people have come to eat, not for a concert. Lyons knows he is background music for most of the customers, though he can almost always look up and see a table of regulars making requests.

"They don't want to be accosted by the music," said Lyons of the patrons. "You're always thinking about how you program your material. Fast, slow. Major, minor.

"There are some nights when nobody's paying attention and that's a pain in the ass, I might as well be home practicing. Sometimes having a noisy crowd is good for concentration." Lyons plays his three-hour-plus sets entirely from memory and while the music will never be intrusive, it will vary in pace considerably, from slow, moody songs to livelier, bouncier ones.

"Sometimes you want to read the comics and sometimes you want to read the editorial page," he said. "I don't think you can play honestly unless you play pieces that you dearly love."

Lyons is considered family at Villa Nova. He walked in one day and owner George Chrimat adopted him. Chrimat used to play classical guitar himself.

"He's a very mellow, nice guitarist," said Chrimat. "A lot of people ask, 'Does Shawn play tonight?' Music with good food goes well, just like a tango. He's got a lot of followers. We love him. I have plenty of respect for him."

Lyons will more readily talk music than snowshoeing. He will pooh-pooh chitchat about sports and even uses one of his Iditashoe trophies that is furniture-like in size as a clothes horse for his workout attire. But he also admits he cares deeply about the race.

"Obviously, it's very special to me," said Lyons. "It's the first sporting event I've ever had any notoriety in."

And just maybe the first one that stripped away enough layers to show him what he's really made of.

In his first Iditashoe in 1986, when he was shepherded home by the Northern Lights, Lyons beat freezing weather, cold rain, and a tough field.

He came upon the last man ahead of him lying beside the trail in a sleeping bag. He could have passed him silently, but instead woke him to check on his health. The man rose and chased him. Lyons considered that possibility, but to Lyons, the code of the wild takes precedence over competition. He had to know the man wasn't in danger before leaving him behind.

The next year Lyons set his record. He wanted to prove the first win was no fluke. He lived on Snickers bars, granola bars, and pound cake. In 1988, the snow was like sand, like running on the beach, and his time was six hours off the record.

Frank Bozanich, now a policeman in Anaktuvuk Pass, a remote Alaskan village, was living in Bothell, Wash., when he first attempted the Iditashoe. He is a winner of six national championships at ultramarathon distances and there was no reason to think running on the road wouldn't translate well to running on snowshoes on the snow. But Bozanich is one of those runners with big-time credentials whom Lyons beat. More than once, in fact. Bozanich discovered running on snowshoes was different.

"It's just that you're going so long through the night and the cold," he said.

He didn't know who Lyons was before, but he knows now, especially after snowshoeing about 20 miles with him one year.

"He seems like a pretty nice guy," said Bozanich. "He just doesn't seem that athletic. The 27 hours, though, that was amazing."

There it is again. Another guy other folks consider amazing calling Lyons amazing. Well, Lyons has some more amazing thoughts for them. If the weather's just right— clear skies and the temperature not dipping too much below zero—he thinks the record can go under 24 hours.

"I think 24 hours is feasible," said Lyons. "In my 27 hours, I spent four hours at the last checkpoint because I was so cold. I wasn't going to leave until the sun came up."

Lyons knows he doesn't have the imposing physique of the athlete and doesn't boast either. But he has proven himself over and over again in the wild.

"If you force us to carry something and go up and down hills, the longer we stay out there, the better I get," he said. "Generally, the rougher the conditions, if it's a wilderness race, I start to excel. I'm surprised I've done so well, to tell you the truth. I think I've developed my slow-twitch muscles to a high degree."

One year the weather will be just right, but in the meantime, Lyons finds other ways to astound his fans and followers. In 1990 the simultaneous Iditashoe and Iditaski races were shortened to 86 miles. Lyons beat all but two Iditaskiers, whose mode of transportation was theoretically faster. Visiting Soviets took the top two places in the race and then came Shawn, trotting into the finish. He was exultant, not solely because he'd clung to his title once more, but because he'd never come close to outslogging the majority of skiers.

"I never thought that would happen," said Lyons. "It's a coup."

Deep snow hindered the pace in that race, too, so Lyons's snowshoe time of 24 hours, 16 minutes wasn't a threat to the 24-hour barrier he had hoped to achieve for the usually longer race.

"I really slowed down the last 18 miles," said Lyons. "I hit the wall. It was real satisfying for the first time to race the skiers, though."

Anything can happen in a long race. And anything can happen in the Alaska wilderness in winter. Lyons knows that there's risk every time he starts a race like the Iditashoe.

"You could get sick," said Lyons. "You can fall down a creek bed."

Or just maybe you get to see the Northern Lights in the northern night.

John Faeo
of Anchorage

No One Can Touch Faeo

A cowboy on the range. Free under the stars, alone in the emptiness of the land, frozen ground a blur beneath him, John Faeo rides. One hundred miles an hour across the barrenness of Interior Alaska, weaving through a forest of bare trees, John Faeo flies on his snowmachine.

Knuckles grip handles white-hard, the body bounces with the terrain. The machine rides with the wind. Faster than the wind.

John Faeo is faster than the wind. And he most certainly is faster than other men. No one's close. John Faeo always gets there first.

He's won the big ones. He's won the little ones. He's won the short ones. He's won the long ones.

He's won the Hatcher Pass 60 seven times. He's won the Talkeetna to Anchorage eight times. He's won the Gold Rush Classic, 1,000 miles between Big Lake and Nome, four times. He's won in Nome. He's won in Valdez. He's won in Kotzebue.

Any time, any place. It's been going on like this for years. Any Alaskan athlete tempted to claim dominance in a sport must hesitate; no one compares to Faeo.

He's well into his 30s and he's been at it since 1973. No one can touch him.

"It's hard to quit on top. I figured I'd quit when the young bloods came up and knocked me off," says Faeo. "It just hasn't happened."

The machine was first a hurtling speck in the distance on Willow Lake, seen before heard. Then, as the dot enlarged, dark against the snow, the machine's roar filled the air before the man could be seen. Soon, as the snowmachine approached the finish line, it was clear: Faeo again.

As Faeo glided the machine to a stop and parked it, the flat, white expanse of the lake tucked into the trees off the highway in the town of Willow remained empty. Second place wasn't in sight. It was the 19th annual Hatcher Pass 60 in February, 1989, and for the seventh time it was Faeo's.

One by one, they straggled in on the sunny, minus-15-degree day. The other members of the Alaska Motor Mushers were greeted by a sight they have long grown accustomed to: a cooled-down Faeo, arms folded, chatting away, wearing a baseball cap. The only thing missing was the cigar. Faeo gave up cigars that year.

Like former Boston Celtics' Coach Red Auerbach, Faeo infuriated his foes with a victory cigar. Faeo smoked those thin, plastic-tipped Swisher Sweets for years. Racers would cross the finish line sweating and see Faeo puffing away.

"It drives the competition crazy," says Faeo, grinning slyly. "They think, 'How long has he been here?' "

Usually, the answer is quite a while. Take Faeo's most recent Hatcher Pass win. Faeo's record run for the 60-mile race from Palmer to Willow over 3,500-foot Hatcher Pass, some 60 miles north of Anchorage, was five minutes shorter than anyone else's.

"How do you beat him?" asks former club president Ken Lee. "You go out and jump in front of him. The man is just part of the machine. He's more machine than human."

Maybe there's something to that. Faeo, a firm six feet and 170 pounds, is a mechanic by trade. He usually has grease under his fingernails. He has worked as a diesel locomotive machinist for the Alaska Railroad in Anchorage since he got out of high school. He flies a Cessna 185 airplane. He devotes 35 or more hours a week to fine-tuning his Polaris 650 snowmachine or his other racing model of the moment. The man is more at home with engine blocks, carburetors, and oil filters than Roger Penske (the Indy 500 owner-manager).

People were shaking their heads at Willow Lake. Faeo started 21st and made up the 30-second staggers on everyone ahead of him.

At the finish, he still had enough time to catch his breath and whip off his colorful red helmet with "Faeo" scripted on the side before any other machine came into the neighborhood.

"I know I could still do that race faster if I went out number one," says Faeo. "You do get hung up a little bit. Sometimes it's 30 seconds, sometimes it's just a few seconds. That all adds up."

Plus, he made a wrong turn and figures that cost him a minute. Hey, no one's perfect.

But most snowmachiners think Faeo is. It's not because he runs, swims, or lifts weights. All of his training, building the muscles in his shoulders, arms, and his grip, come from riding. He may have the best machine, but he thinks the rider's judgment and experience accounts for 70 percent of the success. And this rider is still the best.

"King John. That's what I call him," says race official and frequent racer Andrew Corbin. "King John. I don't think he loses unless he breaks down."

That does happen. Faeo and his partners have won the Gold Rush Classic, also known as the Iron Dog, five of the seven times it has been run. Another time he was second.

In the Gold Rush Classic, the racers switch directions each year, north to south, or south to north along the Iditarod Trail. But whichever direction they choose, armed with a map and compass, they need intuition, too, to dodge mountains and rivers. Thirty miles from Nome in the 1988 race, Faeo developed a suspension problem. His teammate, Rod Frank, hit the finish first, but the team of Scott Davis and Gary Eoff beat Faeo in. Both racers have to finish before the place is calculated.

"It came down to a drag race the last five miles," says Faeo.

But there was nothing to match the 1990 Gold Rush, which was run from Nome to Anchorage in unbelievable, intensely cold temperatures. It was 60 below during the race and combine that temperature with the windchill created by zooming along at high speed and you get a reading that the body can't comprehend, never mind cope with very easily. Every square inch of flesh must be protected or suffer.

"I was prepared, but it takes the fun out of it," says Faeo, who won the race.

Snowmachines resemble Indy 500 cars in delicacy. The $5,000 machines are made to go fast, but they are not necessarily built tough enough to zip across frozen tundra, through felled trees, over snow-coated boulders, for hours or days straight at full throttle, without coming to harm. Sometimes there is time to fix the problem, sometimes there isn't.

Winning has made Faeo a legend over the years. But winning the hard way has enhanced it. His wildest moments will pass into folklore.

In 1982, at the Mayor's Cup in Valdez, Faeo's brakes failed in the first three miles of a 100-mile race.

"I'll never forget that one," he says.

The snowmachine hit a berm, flipped over, and hurled Faeo into the air. He landed face down in the snow and the machine landed on his back. The only reason the 450-pound machine didn't rearrange his spine was because the leather-cushioned seat is the part that hit flush. He got up, climbed back on, and finished the race. He won. With no brakes.

Another time, in the Jack Helms Memorial at Big Lake in 1980, Faeo drove 200 miles with no brakes. They went out in the first mile and he steered safely through four 50-mile loops without a crash. He won, of course.

"He's just so aggressive," says Lee.

Maybe it's not only the cigar that psyches out the competition.

It is love of the country, not the thrill of the speed, that keeps Faeo on snowmachines. It is the wild that makes him feel alive.

Goes back to his boyhood. He grew up in Anchorage, but always escaped to the land. His dad John and mother Betty always took him north to places where the moose, bear and caribou outnumbered people. A snowmachine was the easiest way to see the country.

"He started riding as a young lad and he loves it," says Mrs. Faeo, whose volumes of scrapbooks filled with her son's clippings are like a set of Encyclopedia Britannica.

"They just rode and rode. All day Saturday. All day long."

Faeo was not always unbeatable. Several years ago, in the 1970s, snowmachine racing in the Anchorage area attracted up to 500 riders to race instead of perhaps 30, and it took time to learn to be the best.

Faeo got a taste of that kind of racing once more in the winter of 1990 on a trip to Minnesota. He finished third in the Jeep 500. He had starting place number 170 in the field of 220 sleds and passed 102 of them on the trail. He was two seconds out of second place in elapsed time.

"It was fun," he says of the mob.

When he started racing as a teen in Anchorage, Faeo was just one of the pack, too.

"I was young and dumb," he says. "I used to go fast and not pull back. I didn't always finish, or come in with flying colors. I used to fall off and get back on." Mrs. Faeo fretted about him. A lot. Even though he never broke a bone. Before each race she slipped a religious medal into his pocket for good luck. She still does it.

"It's unnerving," she says. "My skin was jumping and crawling. I thought I'd have a stroke."

Faeo has won a lot of money snowmachine racing over the years, though he's not sure exactly how much. His biggest purse was $17,000, won in the small northwestern Alaska town of Kotzebue, in 1990.

He averaged 80 miles an hour on a very flat course, despite stopping for gas three times.

"It was like driving on the Parks Highway," says Faeo in comparing the very flat surface with the main travelers' road between Anchorage and Fairbanks. "Fifteen times I've been up there. I've never seen it smoother."

He's also made good money in the Gold Rush, but his $5,000 breakthrough came in 1973 in the Wasilla Grand Prix.

"I went out and bought a new car," he says. "I was 17 years old with a brand new car, an AMX. I blew the wad."

Since then Faeo has won so many trophies and plaques, some of them over three feet high, that the basement rec room of his old house was lined with them. They spill out of boxes. If Faeo melted down all the metal in the room, he could probably retire young.

Faeo talks about retirement. Not from work, but from snowmachine racing. He says the other racers ask him all the time when he plans to hang up his leather racing duds. He tells them to pool their money to pay him off.

"I've slowed down," says Faeo. "I've been wanting to get out of this for the last few years."

He says he really wants to spend more time with his family, more time fishing, more time hunting, more time just riding for fun. It is hard to quit, though, when he's still winning all the time, when purses of several thousand dollars beckon. Faeo says winning feeds his ego.

"People keep saying they're going to kick your butt, and they don't," he says. "I don't want somebody else to get what's mine. I used to really enjoy the racing, but the field has shrunk. It's the same old heads."

As long as Faeo can manage to stay hungry, other racers figure, he will still be the best, out of reach of the best challengers.

"You can't get much better than John," says Anchorage racer Bob Brock. "He's like a Chuck Yeager. He will probably never be beaten."

S itting in the living room of his old home — he is building a new one — Faeo looks the part of an outdoorsman. He has a light-colored mustache and dresses in jeans and a flannel shirt. The walls are filled with evidence of the country, skins of animals he and his wife Vicki have hunted. A black bear rug, a brown bear rug, a brown bear head, a raccoon, a sheep head, a wolf.

There is no mistaking the pride in his voice when Faeo talks about his snowmachining accomplishments, but there is no mistaking the joy that lights his whole face when he talks about his cabin in the wild near the small settlement of Skwentna where he retreats with Vicki and his young sons John and Scott.

"It's just beautiful," he says. "You can just go for miles."

The man who goes so fast, who goes so much faster than anyone else, prefers going slow with his boys. The competition would be surprised to hear that. That's like Carl Lewis saying he'd prefer jogging through the park rather than bursting out of the starting blocks.

"I like to go slow, too," says Faeo. "I like to look at the countryside. The cabin is just this side of the Alaska Range. There's no other riding like it. There's always fresh snow."

On the weekends, when he isn't hunting, Faeo flies to the cabin and rides for hours at 30 miles per hour. On sunny days, the view is a clear one of the rising snow-coated peaks of the mountains. It is quiet, but for the sound of the machine skimming over the deep snow.

In these moments, Faeo the snowmachiner isn't Faeo the racer. He is just a man in the wilderness. Just a cowboy on the range.

4
Mountain Highs

Most of the biggest mountains in the United States are in Alaska. There are none approaching 15,000 feet in the other 49 states, while Alaska has plenty of them over 16,000 feet high.

None of those peaks, however, capture the public imagination and attention the way Mount McKinley in the Alaska Range does. McKinley, located deep in Alaska's Interior, is 20,320 feet tall and it is the tallest mountain in North America. People come from all over the country and all over the world to climb it.

There have been many great adventures and many great adventurers linked to McKinley, and the challenges and the dangers it presents. No expedition, though, has ever seemed quite so dramatic as the first winter ascent of the mountain in 1967.

Perhaps because the mountain was still comparatively unexplored, perhaps because the mere idea of trying to cope with the terrible storms such a beast could produce seemed unbelievable to the average person, the story of the first conquest of McKinley in winter lives on in Alaska climbing lore.

McKinley helped make Ray Genet famous. He was one of the three climbers who made that ascent and he kept returning to McKinley's slopes. A romantic figure, he also later died on a mountain climb.

Art Davidson, one of his partners, took a very different path in life after the pioneer ascent, branching off in many different directions.

Harry Johnson, meanwhile, was not one of those three climbers, but eventually became the owner of the guiding business which Genet founded. He has become one of the most diversified adventurers in Alaska, willing to put his body on the line for any great physical challenge.

Ray Genet
of Talkeetna

The Legend of Ray Genet

Their frostbitten hands were almost useless. So cold they were claws. Their toes were numb. So cold they could barely bend. With crumbs for food, fumes for fuel, and without water for 36 hours, Art Davidson, Dave Johnston and Ray Genet sat huddled together in 30-below cold waiting for death to take them.

Trapped by a raging storm in a snow cave at 18,200 feet, just below Mount McKinley's summit, they listened to the roaring wind pile snow at their front door.

There was one hope. Somewhere out there was a buried cache of fuel, fuel to warm them, fuel to melt snow. Somewhere within 200 feet. Who would be brave enough to seek it?

To sit still was to die. Ray Genet moved. With no discussion, he pulled his face mask down and squirmed out of the snow cave. Minutes ticked by. The others wondered. And then 15 minutes after he departed, Genet returned, bearing life in a gas can.

More than 22 years later—22 years after the three men made the first winter ascent of Mount McKinley—Davidson recalled the moment as vividly as if it were then flashing across the television set in his living room.

"I wouldn't be alive today if it weren't for Ray Genet," said Davidson.

Stop time right there. Freeze it, for that is the moment the swashbuckling, daring, colorful legend of Ray Genet began.

Twelve years later, the man who climbed McKinley more times than anyone else, the man who pioneered guiding on North America's highest peak, the seemingly indestructible Ray Genet, died at the age of 48 while descending from the summit of Mount Everest.

"For the legend, for the folklore of Ray Genet, it was right for him to die on Mount Everest," said Harry Johnson, the man who now owns the Genet Expeditions guide service. "It was fitting."

Ray Genet was born Swiss, but he died Alaskan. He died as the undisputed king of Mount McKinley. He made the mountain his personal playground, his special place in the world. And the mountain made his name.

Another decade has passed since Genet died, but the legend lives on.

The Pirate. That was what they called Genet. When the gear was parceled out on the first winter ascent in 1967 he grabbed all the orange stuff for himself—his natural flashiness—and drew a skull and crossbones on it. That's how he earned the nickname. He made the skull and crossbones a trademark. One of many.

The man did not shrink from the spotlight. He sought it, reveled in it, thrived on it. Genet promoted himself with the relentlessness of a presidential advance man. A purple sunset didn't leave you as breathless and awestruck.

The bandana he wore gave him a rakish appearance and hid his spreading baldness. He had a thick, bushy beard and his eyes were glowing coals. He wore leather vests tied with rawhide strips and dangled carabiners from his belt. Transportation was a red Cadillac convertible that he drove with top down when it was 30 below. Genet made an impression.

"Ray was a very, very intense, flamboyant kind of guy. He totally did what he wanted to do and said what he wanted to say. It was 'I'm alive. I'm gonna do what I'm gonna do,' " said Davidson, who lives in the tiny community of Rainbow, just south of Anchorage. "He just met life full on."

Sometimes it was a head-on collision. He was a playboy of the first rank. Women loved him, couldn't resist him. Genet had groupies, female climbing clients who followed him around "like puppy dogs," said Gary Bocarde, who founded a competing guide service on McKinley in 1976.

"He used to kid me that we never had women on our trips and he always had women," said Bocarde. "He'd say, 'God, you got to shape up. C'mon.' "

Genet, it seems, was a Svengali. He'd woo women over the counter in stores. Davidson imitates Genet's manner and French accent. "Ve go to zee summit," he'd say to those girls. Some would get goo-goo eyed and follow him to the mountain.

"Some people would call Ray a user, but I'd say he was satisfying their groupie instincts," said Berkley Tilton, Genet's longtime friend and climbing partner. "He put them on as assistant guides, which meant they were assistant slaves. He always wanted to save a buck. He was conscious of that."

Women also hated him. Genet would sneak up behind women he'd never met, reach around them, and grab them by their breasts. "Aha! Ray Genet!" he'd shout, then laugh.

"If you or I did that, we'd go to jail," said Davidson. "He had an impish charm that enabled him to get away with things."

The Pirate's laugh was a cackle. Sometimes it protected him, sometimes not. Occasionally the women would be feisty. Tilton said he saw Genet squeeze one woman, who responded by grabbing a cast iron frying pan and smacking him on the head.

"He liked to shock, but not to offend," said Tilton. "He especially loved to shock women."

If the woman could take a small dose of Ray Genet, if she could handle his peculiar way of introducing himself, she'd gain his respect. If she matched him, wit for wit, will for will, he was intrigued. If not, she was disposable. Rudeness was a test to see if you had the mettle to be his friend.

"He wanted to associate with people who could take the shock and see beyond it," said Tilton, now a real estate developer in Wasilla, north of Anchorage, but who then lived next door to Genet in Talkeetna, the town of about 400 people that in spring and summer serves as the jumping-off point for the international crowd of climbers who come to Alaska to challenge McKinley.

Roni Hale, also from Talkeetna, whose husband Jim was an assistant guide for Genet, said, "I don't think he had a lot of respect for the women's race. He treated all women pretty much the same, but some of the women were able to have a comeback."

Those were the women whom Genet stuck with and who stuck with him. He had three children, Saskia, a girl now 22, from a previous relationship, and two boys — Taurus, 12, and Adrien, 10 — by Kathy Sullivan of Talkeetna, who was with him during the last years of his life. In between, there were many others bewitched by the boldness of a man who dared to live his life like a pirate.

"He had an attitude of 'I'm up in the mainsail and I'm going to any corner of the world I like.' Women were attracted to him, but men were, too," said Davidson, who said he considered Genet a brother. "He was a romantic figure, larger than life."

Not at first, though. Until Ray Genet met Mount McKinley, he was a painter without a canvas, a genius with no forum to express himself. Without McKinley, Genet would likely have been an unknown eccentric. McKinley gave him a stage.

"He became Ray Genet at the age of 36," said Davidson, "the Ray Genet people looked up to. He found his calling in life."

Proud men with big dreams have had big moments on the forbidding McKinley slopes that stretch 20,320 feet into the sky. But no name is as linked to the symbol of Alaskan wilderness as Genet.

He dominated it in the same manner he dominated starry-eyed girls — through force of will. Genet stood on the summit of Mount McKinley no less than 25 times and perhaps as many as 45 times. No one is quite sure because the National Park Service didn't keep records in the late 1960s and early 1970s when Genet became the first to guide citizen climbers.

Genet helped make climbing McKinley popular. More than 1,000 people attempted to climb the mountain in 1990, but until Genet made the West Buttress route his personal highway, few but hard-core adventurers tried it.

Genet did not simply climb McKinley. Having the lungs of an Olympic marathon runner allowed him to dash up and down it.

Assistant guides would start the clients on the mountain. Slowly, over a period of several days, they'd work their way up the mountain to 14,000 feet or so. Genet would fly into the Kahiltna Glacier at 7,200 feet and catch up to them in one day. Then he'd lead the climbers to the summit, run halfway down the mountain, and lead another group to the top. Strong men in their own right marveled at his strength.

"He had trips that would have 20 people, mass trips, a cast of thousands," said Bocarde. "He was strong, he was definitely strong." How strong was he? More powerful than a man who was 5-foot-8 and 160 pounds had a right to be.

"He was one of the strongest men I've ever seen for his size," said Joe Redington, the cofounder of the Iditarod Trail Sled Dog Race. In 1979, Genet guided Redington, Susan Butcher, and a team of dogs to the top of McKinley.

Genet was not a famous climber before the winter ascent of McKinley. He was no Edmund Hillary, no technical wonder. He was even a latecomer to that pioneer group and had to talk his way onto the expedition.

The trip was all set. All of the climbers had signed on and the organizers weren't shopping for any more bodies. Then Davidson began getting phone calls from Genet, trying to convince him that an expedition without Ray Genet was no expedition at all. Genet was selling not only himself, but a French friend, Jacques Batkin. Batkin was well known. In the end, Davidson said, the group relented because of Batkin's name, but Davidson also admired Genet's spunk and persuasiveness.

"He wouldn't take no for an answer," said Davidson.

As it turned out, the climb that made Genet famous, was also Batkin's last. Batkin was killed early on the trip when he fell into a crevasse.

Talk was certainly a Genet forte. He cited cross-country skiing and climbs of several peaks in the Alps to Davidson as credentials.

"We didn't realize until later that you can drive to the top of most of them," said Davidson, who chuckles with warmth as he notes that.

He also laughs at one of his first visions of Genet on McKinley. The climbers were at the Kahiltna Glacier base camp. Davidson awoke to the sounds of huffing and puffing and grunts. Genet was running in place and doing jumping jacks.

Genet had knocked around. He had worked construction, done some carpentry and house painting. In the 1950s, Genet had sold real estate during a boom in Montreal wore a jacket and tie to work, something people who knew him later find difficult to believe.

"He didn't really fit in a lot of places," said Davidson. "He could never have worked in an office."

Actually, Genet was hustling real estate more on the street than in an office and that job honed his aggressiveness and salesmanship.

Genet was always trying to make his mark, make his point, by sheer willpower. Bocarde remembers laughing as he came upon Genet kicking the hell out of a recalcitrant stove at 14,000 feet on McKinley.

"That's what he'd do with mechanical things when they didn't work," said Bocarde.

He would order pilots around, too, try to get them to operate on his schedule rather than their own. Famed bush pilot Lowell Thomas, Jr. was new to McKinley in 1979 so he was flexible, trying to get more business, and he thinks that's one reason Genet sought his services.

Thomas's last flight for Genet in July, 1979, illustrated Genet's demanding nature, his impatience, and his knowledge of McKinley.

Thomas received a radio call from the mountain. It was Genet. "Thomas, we're coming down tonight," Thomas recalls Genet saying. "Can you be there at 6 o'clock in the morning?"

Thomas was there and flew Genet's party back to Talkeetna. Then the weather closed in and other parties who waited for more civilized business hours got stranded on the mountain for several days. "The early bird got the worm and the others got the weather," said Thomas.

Because Genet was the first and had virtually invented an industry, he became possessive of the mountain, jealous of other guides. He saw McKinley as his mountain and that caused friction. Bocarde said Genet didn't speak to him the first year he guided, though they later became friends.

Michael Covington, a Colorado-based guide who has climbed McKinley five different ways — more than anyone else — said Genet initially viewed him with suspicion because he saw him as a competitor. When Genet realized Covington was more interested in routes on the mountain other than the West Buttress, he welcomed Covington.

"He was really a warm, good-hearted person when you got to know him," said Covington. "But you could certainly get on the wrong side of him. When you got close to him, he trusted you."

Many guides did eventually come to McKinley, but no one imposed his will on climbers the way Genet did. "To zee summit! To zee summit!" That was Genet's rallying cry.

You came to climb a mountain and, by God, Ray Genet would get you to the top — grunting and wheezing, if need be. If Genet felt a tongue-lashing would move you, you got whipped. If a prick with an ice ax would move you, you got stuck. If a kick in the rear end would make you step, you got booted.

Genet seemed to think the clients should be as driven as he was. Friends say Genet had an authoritarian father and that his drive stemmed from desire to show his dad he could be successful. Genet often made the clients angry so they'd want to show him they could succeed. Redington said Genet was a great psychologist, who could look inside a person and sense what it would take to motivate them.

"He could be a bear," agreed Kathy Sullivan, who worked as an assistant guide for Genet, "but he could be incredibly delicate and gentle."

That was a side of Genet that the public rarely saw. Those who knew him best say he could be warm, caring, and was always there for friends in need. Once, a Talkeetna couple's cabin burned down and he spent seven hours comforting them.

Genet's safety record was good. Only one client died on a Genet climb, of a heart attack, after Genet only reluctantly let him continue. Still, his style was controversial and made people wonder about the risks being taken.

Jim Hale quit guiding for him in an angry huff because he believed Genet's judgment was clouded by his quest for getting clients to the summit.

On his last trip with Genet in 1974, he and another assistant guide turned back a party of 25 at 14,000 feet because of avalanche danger. Genet met the group on the Kahiltna Glacier and wanted to go back up. Hale refused.

"That was when he told me he had made a decision never to turn around," said Hale. "It was always to the summit, no matter what."

It took a few years for the wounds from that blowup to heal. Hale became a pastor and said he came to understand that gruff exteriors often mask more sensitive interiors. "I really liked him," he said. "He was a very unique person. You either loved him or hated him." The two eventually became friends again.

Tilton, who climbed McKinley with Genet four times, said climbers used to come with a spiritual vision of

McKinley's mystique. There they were in the wild, in Alaska, making dreams of a lifetime come true. Genet cut through the romance of their imagery with plain words. Climbing a big, mean mountain was hard work.

"His philosophy was that love never put anybody on the summit," said Tilton. "Hate did. If he couldn't get them to hate the mountain, he'd get them to hate him. It worked. I saw it."

All Alaska saw it. And maybe they did hate Genet for a time, but by the time they were flying out with Thomas, many were praising Genet.

"They'd say, 'He got us up and that's what we paid him to do,' " said Thomas.

Could Genet survive and thrive in this age of increased National Park Service regulation, when guide services are plentiful and clients are more often than not upscale, white-collar workers on a three-week vacation?

"He certainly would have been an interesting character to work with if you were in my shoes," said Bob Seibert, the chief McKinley ranger. "If Ray was still in power, if you will, it would have been interesting. He pretty much had a free rein."

Today's clients expect to be coddled more, said Harry Johnson, who bought Genet Expeditions from Sullivan in 1983. These days on non-McKinley trips in other parts of the world, the climbers also go to the beach and stay at fancy hotels.

"Genet wasn't a diplomat," said Johnson, who met Genet for the first and only time while on a 1976 McKinley climb.

"Today, in the baby boomer age, there are massive numbers of people. Today, you have to baby your clients more.

"I can't really picture Ray sitting in the hotel eating the buffet. Maybe he would have mellowed, but I don't think so. I wouldn't have wanted him to."

U̲p and down the mountain. The spring of 1979 was the same as all of the other springs of the previous decade for Ray Genet. His home was McKinley. But McKinley was beginning to wear him out. Too much time up high. Too much time in the cold. Too many ups and downs.

"He was incredibly tired that year," said Sullivan.

Sullivan was clearly the special woman in Genet's life, "an Olympic caliber woman," according to Roni Hale, who could heft 90-pound packs, who could toss Genet himself over her shoulders. A woman, said Bocarde, as strong-willed as Genet.

The weariness was so deep Genet talked often of ending his love affair with McKinley, selling the business, and settling down with Kathy and the kids. Maybe he'd buy a sailboat and take to the seas.

"He talked of packing up the oatmeal and sugar and taking off across Canada and Alaska," said Sullivan. "It was a matter of change."

Genet had developed a persistent, hacking cough, and chronic bronchitis, from the cold and fatigue. But he refused to slow down, refused to stop pushing. He was already exhausted when the invitation to climb Everest, at 29,028 feet the tallest mountain in the world, came from a West German group.

How does a man who has built a name as a great mountaineer refuse the chance to climb the world's greatest mountain? How does a man who has never said no to a summit say no to the world's grandest summit? Yet, from all accounts, recognizing his fatigue, Genet did seriously consider refusing to dance this dance.

"There was a big question of whether he wanted to go or not," said Sullivan. "He felt he needed to and he felt he didn't need to."

In May of that year, Michael Covington bumped into Genet at about 12,000 feet on the West Buttress. He remembers Genet making hot chocolate for him and telling him both how tired he was and about his opportunity to go to Everest.

Covington had climbed in the Himalayas. "I said, 'Ray, it's my experience if you don't feel 100 percent going in, don't go. Those mountains are too high and too dangerous."

Covington said Genet looked at him and said, "Yeah, I know that, but it's Everest."

All spring and most of the summer, Genet vacillated. Back and forth. One minute he was going, the next minute not. He said he was too tired, then he said it was the chance of a lifetime and a chance to show he was more than a one-mountain wonder.

Tilton had witnessed Genet's coughing up close on climbs. He advised him not to go to Nepal.

"Ray would be the first one to admit he killed himself," said Tilton. "I told him he was stupid. I told him, 'You're totally stupid for going. You'll get another chance.'"

Everyone who saw Genet in the weeks leading up to the Everest trip walked away with a similar impression. His friends all knew he was a tired man. The last time Thomas ever saw Genet, it was over dinner in Anchorage. Thomas still remembers Genet as looking haggard. "He didn't have a chance to rest up," said Thomas. "I guess he just ran out of steam."

Thomas recalls Genet's parting thought: " 'I'm gonna go for the big one.' "

The day before Genet's departure, the Hales ran into him at the Three Rivers Gas Station in Talkeetna.

"His eyes were sunken and he was coughing," said Jim Hale. "I don't think he really wanted to go on another cold, high mountain."

But Genet went, even though the expedition had started trekking in to Everest base camp while he was still in Alaska. Soon after arriving in Nepal, he got sick and was hospitalized in the village of Khumde. That gave Genet another chance to withdraw from the expedition. He chose to go on.

"He felt it was an opportunity and a challenge and he had to do it," said Sullivan. "So destiny takes effect."

Sullivan had remained in Talkeetna, but Genet sent a telegram asking her to join him. Sullivan was six months pregnant during her own days-long march to Everest base camp. A sherpa carried Taurus, then less than two.

Sullivan had no premonition Genet was in danger, but the whole time trekking in to the mountain base camp the lyrics to Led Zeppelin's "Stairway to Heaven" pounded in her head:

> *"There's a lady who's sure all that glitters is gold.*
> *And she's buying a stairway to heaven.*
> *And when she gets there she knows*
> *If the stores are closed*
> *With a word she can get what she came for.*

Sullivan never got what she came for. When she reached base camp at 18,000 feet, Genet was already climbing.

Covington was there with a British expedition about to climb Nuptse, a 25,726-foot mountain just to the north of Everest. Covington was shocked at Genet's appearance in base camp. "He looked a mess," said Covington. "It doesn't even look like Ray. He just looked old and haggard."

The two friends talked. Covington said Genet told him, "Boy, I don't know what to do. I've been really sick."

"I told him, 'You look completely wiped. It's your decision, but I'd probably stay if it was me.' "

Covington went to sleep. When he awoke, Genet was gone, already somewhere on the slopes of Everest.

In the days that followed, Genet, the man of immense stamina, called upon every ounce of his determination to overpower his weariness and carry himself to the top of the world.

On the way down from the summit, the body that craved rest ran out of energy. With no oxygen, no tents, and no sleeping bags, Genet, Hannelore Schmatz, the wife of the expedition leader, and a sherpa, Sundare, made an emergency camp outdoors at 28,000 feet. They were about three hours above Camp IV, which offered more protection. Sometime during the night, Genet froze to death. The next day, Schmatz collapsed and died, too. Sundare survived.

At base camp, the radio crackled. Reports were sketchy. Nepalese soldiers at first said everyone was dead. Then they said everyone was OK. No one was sure. Finally, Sundare returned with the truth.

Covington was staggered when he learned Genet was dead. Then he steeled himself. He knew he must tell Sullivan.

They moved away from the heart of the camp and sat on a rock. Sullivan made idle chitchat, and then she saw Covington's face. "He's gone, isn't he?" she asked him. Covington nodded.

Back in Alaska, those who knew Ray Genet, those who saw him as a Paul Bunyan, could not believe he was dead.

Berkley Tilton's first thought was, "They've screwed up the goddamn news release."

Davidson read about Genet in the morning newspaper. "I was just stunned and tears came to my eyes," he said.

They had all warned Genet, told him not to go, but they knew that once he'd left, he'd never give in to his gnawing fatigue.

"It was not in him to turn back," said Davidson. "It was not in his nature to give up on something. Ray Genet was always the one who got people to the summit."

No, Ray Genet couldn't turn back. Not once the Pirate set the mainsail for a summit. Even if it killed him.

Rarely have a man and a mountain, been better matched, rarely have one man and one mountain been a better team. Genet and McKinley. McKinley and Genet.

"The time, the era, and the mountain and what could be done; he was made for it," said Tilton.

Sullivan hasn't climbed on McKinley in years. One thing could draw her back, however, she said. If the boys want to climb, she will take them; she will go with them. "I would love to do that," she said.

Ten years after his death, a memorial service was held for Genet in Talkeetna. A quiet gathering of friends. He was remembered in many ways, but in one way that infuriates Tilton. Some people said that as long as he was going to die, Genet would have wanted to die on a big mountain like Everest.

Poppycock, said Tilton. "Ray always felt that the dumbest thing a climber could do was die on a mountain," he said. "He wanted to die in bed at 110 years old, screwing some 21-year-old chick."

But Genet didn't. He died on Mount Everest. The snow blew violently the day after Genet died and buried his body. It has never been found.

Some day, perhaps, some weakened climber, his spirit flagging, will pause for rest on the frozen slopes of Everest. A voice will come to him, urging him onwards. "To zee summit!" He will start in surprise and ask, "Who's there?"

The voice will answer with a cackle. And then the words, "Aha! Ray Genet."

Art
Davidson
of Rainbow

Davidson Still Loves the Country

The number alone conjures an image so stark, so chilling, so overwhelming, that most people cannot comprehend it. Minus 148 degrees.

It is difficult to imagine air so cold, so savage, existing anywhere on earth, never mind existing in it, surviving it. Yet that number was not an abstract concept, but a very real threat of death for the men who first climbed Mount McKinley in the winter.

For 42 days, from late January well into March, 1967, eight men challenged the highest peak in North America. One man died. Others suffered frostbite. There were scars, but in the end, there was also triumph; the first winter scaling of the forbidding, 20,320-foot mass of glaciated ice that looms over the Alaska Range as a fierce and proud symbol of Alaska's wilderness.

One of the those climbers was a young Art Davidson, who had come to Alaska from Colorado. He made it to the summit and he made it down from the mountain, to safety in Anchorage. Then he wrote the story of the expedition and called it *Minus 148*.

"At 22 I came to regard the first exploration of Mount McKinley in the winter as a journey into an unexplored land," wrote Davidson. "No one had lived on North America's highest ridges in the winter twilight. No one knew how low the temperatures would drop, or how penetrating the cold could be when the wind blew. For thousands of years, McKinley's winter storms had raged by themselves."

As a child, Davidson did not appear to be a candidate for this type of pioneer exploration.

As a fifth or sixth grader at camp in Wyoming, he met his first mountain, not a particularly tall or daunting one, and all he could think about was falling off.

"I could visualize falling and how one could tear one's body up terribly," says Davidson. "This was not a world-class mountain. At that age, I already had a great love of the mountains, but I had this keen awareness of danger, too."

In high school, Davidson was introduced to rock climbing and discovered what that could be about.

"I found out you had to climb up these little ledges," he says. "I did it with knees shaking and thinking, 'I'll never do this again.' "

Little did he know.

Art Davidson is well into his 40s now and lives in Rainbow in the hills just outside of Anchorage. In the more than two decades since the first winter ascent of Mount Mc-

Kinley, he has been a writer, lecturer, filmmaker, businessman, photographer, and he has campaigned for wilderness protection. His mountaineering book was reprinted not long ago and is again widely available.

He is a tall man, over six feet, and sturdy, with broad shoulders. But he has the gentlest of demeanors. He says he has led a life that has taken him rather than one that was in any way preordained or specifically mapped out. One thing has merely led to another.

His joy in the outdoors led to his climbing career. The climb of McKinley led to his writing. His experience as a backpacker and the pleasure he found in camping out led him to become a conservationist who fought against timber cutting near Anchorage, and for the creation of the Chugach State Park, which abuts Anchorage, more than 20 years ago.

"Just caring about it led me into conservation work," says Davidson.

And being a noted outdoorsman led to his being hired to help a film crew make a documentary on the first ascent of Mount Seattle in the Wrangell-St. Elias Range in Southeast Alaska. Although inexperienced, he got to shoot some of the film and it became award-winning material. Davidson moved into documentary filmmaking and worked for the producers of "Wild Kingdom."

Always, there was passion about the outdoors, being part of it, recording impressions of it, being in it, and making sure it was preserved.

Whatever else he does, though, the name Art Davidson is forever linked to that first winter ascent. If a man is once a senator, the title is attached to his name permanently. It is the same with Davidson.

But once having climbed McKinley in this spectacular fashion, Davidson did not continue taking big risks on big mountains. For almost all of these last two decades, in fact, he has shied away from challenging big mountains, instead drawing his pleasures in the outdoors from smaller scale hikes and climbs in Alaska.

"Many of my most cherished experiences in the mountains have been private," says Davidson. "In a sense, nothing in my life can compare to McKinley. It's the only time in my life I've ever lain in one place for a week and I didn't know if I'd live or die.

"I never felt like I was in competition when I was climbing mountains. Other climbs are every bit as important to me."

None were quite as significant, however. Early in the McKinley climb, Jacques "Farine" Batkin fell into a crevasse and died. Later, after Davidson, Dave Johnston, who in 1986 would try a winter solo ascent of McKinley, and Ray "Pirate" Genet, who became a legendary Alaska climber, reached the summit, they were pinned down by raging winds and snow at 18,000-foot high Denali Pass. Separated from the rest of the team, they dug a snow cave.

"We agreed that the wind coming out of the northwest was funneling through the pass at at least 130 miles per hour," wrote Davidson. "We remembered that a wind of such velocity, combined with the minus-30 to minus-45 air temperature outside our cave, created an equivalent windchill temperature somewhere off the end of the chart; the last figure on the chart was minus 148."

They huddled against uncertainty with little food and limited protection.

"Our companions gave us up for dead," says Davidson, recalling his emotions. "It was a prolonged period of facing death. That has left a permanent effect or influence on my life. Suddenly you realize there are a lot of things in the world you take for granted. You realize how wonderful it is to be alive, just to walk around, to take a breath, to look at trees."

To be the first at anything coveted is special. It's something no one can ever take away. More than 20 years later, Mount McKinley is assaulted by about 1,000 people each climbing season. But there is no crowd in the winter. Not even the accomplished mountaineers, who have admiration for the first winter climb, wish to emulate the feat.

"I think it was pretty amazing," says Todd Miner.

Miner, a mountaineering instructor at the University of Alaska Anchorage, has climbed McKinley twice and has climbed major mountains in South America.

"I'm not crazy enough to go up there in winter," he says. "It's something to really test oneself. You're starting out with the odds against you. That kind of cold really takes a toll on the best climbers."

Geoff Radford of Anchorage has climbed McKinley and all over the world. He reached over 24,000 feet on Gasherbrum IV in the Baltoro Glacier region of Pakistan.

"The climb took a lot of patience and gutsing it out," says Radford. "Those guys certainly had a lot of determination. It's a depressing time of year to climb. It's certainly a hard-core thing to do."

It was a hard-core thing even to train for. During runs, Davidson carried snow in his bare hands. He took his sleeping bag outdoors in Fairbanks in minus-40-degree cold.

After reaching the summit, Davidson, Genet, and Johnston were flown off the mountain, all with frostbite. Davidson spent eight weeks in a wheelchair and six more weeks on crutches.

The world tends to look different at 45 than it does when you're 22. Davidson was part of the notable pioneer climb of McKinley in the same year he also climbed to the top of Mount Logan in Canada, Mount Sanford in the St. Elias Range, and Mount Marcus Baker, tallest mountain in the Chugach Range near Anchorage. It may sound peculiar, but he says he was not a driven person, even then.

"I was aware I was climbing a number of mountains," he says, "but it was this incredible sense of the unknown. It was just this excitement of exploration. It was just terribly, terribly exciting. You're there and it was like Lewis and Clark. I had a lot of energy and the mountains were a great outlet."

Davidson's undiminished appreciation of the mountains' beauty has lingered.

"I'm not doing that same type of thing," says Davidson. "But I have the same sense of excitement about the country, the light, the mountain. It's a relationship with the country."

The mountains, The Mountain, remain, of course, and the view on the horizon proved a powerful lure. Davidson's special relationship with McKinley eventually won out. In July, 1988, Davidson at last returned to McKinley. He went with then-19-year-old Dylan, one of his two sons, as part of a larger climbing group.

Davidson likened the experience to going back to the old neighborhood where you grew up, looking for the fishing hole where you played as a young boy.

He says he didn't even care if he didn't make the summit that time. Just being in the peaceful, white world of McKinley was enough.

The beauty was as he remembered. They hadn't paved over the old fishing hole and built an apartment house.

And Davidson and Dylan both made the summit.

At an autograph appearance for his latest book — *In the Wake of the* Exxon Valdez — a friend snuck up behind Davidson and joked, "Another trashy novel, Art?"

Although Davidson was famous long ago as a writer, he never truly set out to be a writer. Now, as he approaches 50, he is becoming as prolific with a pen as he was as a young mountaineer.

Over the past few years, his byline has appeared frequently in Alaska Magazine, the most prominent monthly publication in the state and one with a national audience. And other works have appeared on bookshelves, including *Alakshak, the Great Land,* an immense coffee table book which Davidson jokes weighs about 15 pounds. This features Davidson's essays accompanying colorful Alaskan scenic pictures.

"It was a chance to get back to parts of Alaska and share and give back through my writing the feelings and beauty of living in this country," he says.

Even more recently, his *Exxon Valdez* book appeared. It is one view of the tremendously damaging oil spill which occurred in Prince William Sound in 1989.

Some 20 years ago when hearings were being conducted on the advisability of building a pipeline through Alaska, Davidson testified about the potential dangers to the environment. He felt certain that the coming of oil would tamper with the health and survival of the land he so loved.

When the *Exxon Valdez* crashed into a reef as it left the port of Valdez about midnight on the day of the disaster, spilling almost 11 million gallons of oil into the pristine waters close to shore, Davidson says, his first reaction was denial. He didn't want to believe the bad news, didn't want to think it could be true.

"I just felt stunned," he says.

His next reaction was to rush to the scene. He had to see what had happened, had to understand what went wrong. That's the story he tried to tell in his book. What went wrong, what they did to his country. His home, Alaska, had been slimed and Davidson had been slimed and Davidson had to be there to defend it.

It will always be that way for Davidson.

"You've just got to have a passion for what you're doing," he says.

If the cause is saving Alaska, it is certain that Art Davidson will be there fighting for that cause.

Harry Johnson
of Anchorage

Pushing the Body Well Past Its Limits

Columbus long ago proved the world isn't flat, but somehow Harry Johnson III has spent his entire life living on the edge.

There are few limits in Harry's world. Only endless horizons. Johnson can see as far as the muscles in his body and the ideas in his head can take him.

To Mount McKinley, the highest point in North America. Johnson has been there five times. To Mount Kilimanjaro in Africa, Aconcagua in Argentina, Mount Elbrus in the Soviet Union, the highest peaks on three other continents. Johnson has been there. To marathons and ultramarathons. Johnson has been there. To 250-mile bicycle rides. Johnson has done that. To the Hawaii Iron

Man Triathlon. And even to Tasmania, the far end of the world, to run and sail against the clock in personally uncharted territories.

Put together all the megalength sporting events Johnson has done and you'd have enough sweat to fill one of the Great Lakes.

If the law of natural selection is truly survival of the fittest, Harry Johnson will be one of the last people left on Earth—presumably still running, still pedaling, still climbing.

"Anybody who's looking for challenges in this world, they don't have to look far," Johnson said.

Challenges. Johnson finds them. He will tell you he's neither possessed nor obsessed, but in the next breath he will talk about climbing Mount Everest. Or about bicycling across the United States. Or running a marathon a month for a year. Or a sub-10-hour Hawaii Iron Man Triathlon, one of his current goals. The man has more goals than Wayne Gretzky. Talking to Harry Johnson can leave you breathless. A body can burn calories just listening to him.

Johnson, now in his mid-30s, has lived in the Anchorage area since age 12. He was an all-conference football free safety and ran high hurdles on the track for Dimond High, so he's pretty much always been involved in sports. Until 1988, though, his name was rarely seen in the results of 10-kilometer runs, bike races, or triathlons. Harry Johnson was busy with other things.

He owns Genet Expeditions, the mountain guiding service he purchased from the heirs of famed McKinley guide Ray Genet. Mountain climbing was his first endurance sport.

Johnson never climbed much until he was 18. That was the year he married Diane, his high school sweetheart, and the year he and some friends decided it would be fun to scale 20,320-foot Mount McKinley. Johnson and his three friends were all 18 or 19. They didn't really know what they were doing, either.

Johnson met Genet in Talkeetna, before leaving for the mountain, and on the mountain itself. Johnson said Genet called them "The Anchorage Kids."

"He looked us over to see if we were fit enough for the mountain," said Johnson. "He probably felt these kids didn't belong on the mountain."

It was true that Johnson and his friends did not fully appreciate the danger.

"It was an absolute miracle we didn't die," said Johnson.

They didn't die. They made the summit. And that wasn't the first time people who know Johnson shook their heads over his exploits.

A year later, in 1976, Harry and Diane jumped in their car and drove from Anchorage to Mexico to climb the three major Mexican volcanoes that are the third, fifth, and seventh highest peaks in North America. The highest, Orizaba, is more than 18,000 feet high.

Another couple, equally short on climbing experience, joined them.

"We were relatively insane," said Johnson.

Johnson picked the volcanoes because they were the only high mountains he could afford to climb. But the adventure marked the emergence of Harry Johnson, animal athlete.

In 1978, he climbed Canada's Mount Logan, the second tallest mountain in North America. The world's highest places have beckoned ever since.

Johnson is never done, never satisfied. His 1989 challenge was to complete the Iron Man Triathlon—a 2.4-mile swim, 112-mile bike ride, and 26.2-mile-run—in less than 10 hours. He was already the fastest Alaskan over the full

Iron Man distance, and that kind of time would put him among the elite triathletes.

"If you can go up Mount McKinley and endure 10 days in a storm, you can put up with 10 hours in the Iron Man," said Johnson.

He finished in 10:14. It was a good time, but he did not reach his goal. But that didn't mean he didn't enjoy the race.

What others think of as harrowing, Johnson considers fun. As part of his preparation, he and Anchorage — training partner Behzad Rajabian bicycled 250 miles from the entrance of Denali National Park to Anchorage in 12 hours.

"Part of what makes them fun is how fast you can cover that distance," he said.

In 1988, Johnson and Laddie Shaw, another training partner, ran the Mountain View to Government Hill 10-kilometer run in Anchorage and then ran from Anchorage to the Eagle River Visitors Center and back, 48 more miles.

"Harry and I enjoy that kind of stuff," said Shaw, a state trooper who now lives in Sitka.

Has anybody suggested that they were crazy?

"Oh, it's been mentioned," said Shaw, who on an afternoon he knew Johnson was being interviewed appeared at the window outside Johnson's first-floor title insurance office and pressed his face to it — wearing a clown mask.

Johnson and Shaw have done crazier endurance things together. In April, 1990, they were invited to join a Seattle sailing crew as the only U.S. team in the Health Australia Three Peaks Race in Tasmania.

Some race. Especially for landlubbers. In this beaut of a race, teams consist of three sailors and two runners. The crew steers the boat 317 nautical miles between ports and then the runners get off and run up and down three different mountains, a total of 78 miles in legs of 38, 20, and 20 miles.

"It was like a marathon a day," said Johnson. But hardly the only problem.

Sailing somewhere in the Bay of Storm (not named by accident, it turned out) as 40-knot winds lashed the yacht and the seas crested at over 20 feet, Johnson thought he was going to die.

"I was probably more afraid than I ever was on Mount McKinley," he said.

Johnson didn't really know what to expect on that adventure. He and Shaw didn't count on visiting with wild boars or tripping over snakes. When they were warned about those dangers, they chuckled, figuring the locals were teasing them.

Wrong. It was all for real.

"I'd say overall, when you look at the running and sailing, it's the hardest race I've ever done," said Johnson.

On the first running leg, up dirt roads at first, into the middle of nowhere after that, the partners nearly bumped into a wild boar. Then Johnson hurdled a snake.

They returned to the boat and pushed off, but for the next 30 hours were tossed by waves and were unable to sleep. They were cramped below-decks and never could regain their energy when it came time to run the second leg.

Welcome to the Tasmanian jungle. The trail was a now-you-see-it, now-you-don't affair, and when they didn't see it, they bushwhacked their way through. About an hour into the course, Johnson was running along and suddenly saw a large mammal out of the corner of his eye. Startled, he jumped back. A kangaroo bounded out of the brush and hopped away into the woods.

"I think Shaw just about died laughing," said Johnson.

About four hours into that run, Johnson and Shaw were striding along a gravel road that led back to the boat. Dusk was falling. Suddenly, Shaw shouted "Snake!" Right on the road in front of them.

"I screamed and jumped about 12 feet," said Johnson. "Especially having already seen a snake."

It turned out this snake was a rope.

And then came the violent boat ride to Hobart for the final run. The boat was constantly buffeted and the runners became sailors fighting to keep it from capsizing. No rest at all on this stretch.

"We were all trashed," said Johnson.

Johnson and Shaw finished second among the 28 running teams, but when combined with the sailors' efforts, they were only 14th overall.

However, the duo did receive the sportsmanship award. Completing the final portion of the run into Hobart, they stopped to don silly masks. That got some howls from the crowd and probably swayed the judges in giving the award.

The prize was a 20-year-old bottle of brandy. There was just one problem. Neither Johnson nor Shaw drink.

Johnson is a man for all seasons. Or, at least, for all activities. As a husband, the father of Heidi and Kristin, two girls under 12, as a climber, runner, and biker, owner of Genet and president of TransAlaska Title Insurance Co., Johnson crisscrosses many worlds.

He's terminally enthusiastic about them all. He comes across as both a levelheaded businessman and one willing to take risks. Take his purchase of Genet Expeditions. Genet was a flamboyant, sometimes controversial figure. Johnson was urged by friends to change the name of the company.

"That was a tough one," said Johnson. "Many people thought of Genet as an arrogant SOB. He wasn't the most liked guy in the Alaska climbing community.

"All my climbing buddies said, 'You should change the name, Harry.'"

But Johnson went with his instincts over the advice; and has never regretted it.

"My opinion was that by keeping the name you maintained a tie to the history of McKinley. He was king of the mountain. Fifteen years ago that was a positive thing and I saw a certain amount of advertising value in maintaining the relationship there.

"One reason people still know about Ray Genet is Genet Expeditions. His name is continually in front of the public. He's a special guy and he deserves a special place in the history of Mount McKinley. He was the pioneer guide on McKinley."

It is Johnson's first inclination to say that the colorful, publicity-seeking Genet and he are so different that Genet couldn't imagine a pinstriped guy like Johnson running the business that bears his name.

"If he knew that a white-collar, family businessman was running his company, he'd turn over in his grave," said Johnson.

But then Johnson rethinks that statement in light of his own exploits, his own wild adventures.

"He and I are as different as night and day, but maybe we're more alike than I think," said Johnson.

Talk to Johnson's friends and acquaintances about him and you hear the same words over and over: positive, upbeat, friendly.

Larry Seethaler is a veteran Anchorage runner who has recently gotten to know Johnson at races. "He's really a congenial guy," he said. "He's got his head screwed on right. He doesn't have a big ego."

Vernon Tejas, the Anchorage mountaineer who became the first man to survive a solo winter ascent of Mount McKinley, is a Genet guide and has worked for Johnson for years, first as a counselor at a kids' wilderness summer camp Johnson founded.

Tejas said he realized Johnson was a wild and crazy guy years ago on a large group hike. They came to a lake near O'Malley Peak, one of the 5,000-foot mountains adjacent to Anchorage. The lake still had ice floating on the surface. Tejas and Johnson were the only ones to jump in.

"The attitude that typifies him for me," said Tejas, "is if you're not going forward, you're going backward."

There's no question Johnson is in perpetual motion and that his preferred direction is forward. He says he likes to stay busy, but he's also retained his perspective.

"He's not out of control," said Dick Jabs, Johnson's swim coach and triathlon trainer. "I've seen people who are unbalanced. I think his values are intact."

By values, Jabs means Johnson's commitment to his businesses and the time he spends with his family despite training a minimum of three hours daily.

"When it gets too obsessive, I have to put my foot down," said Johnson's wife Diane.

Mostly, though, she is supportive.

"I think my life would be boring if he was any other way," said Diane. "I think I'd be bored to death if I had an eight-to-five husband who came home and just wanted dinner."

How does Harry avoid boredom? Let us count the ways.

Well, there was the time he carried then-6-year-old Kristin up to 17,000 feet on Mount Kilimanjaro on his shoulders.

And the time he ran the Boston Marathon in a personal best time of 2 hours, 39 minutes in April, 1989, and then followed up with another marathon the following weekend in 2:45.

"It's not very bright," said Johnson of the back-to-back marathons. Maybe not, but he did it twice during 1989.

He also ran the Pikes Peak Marathon, up to an elevation of 14,110 feet.

And he parasailed off Mount McKinley from 16,400 feet a few years ago.

That one was a doozy. The wind was blasting and Johnson had to be held in place before spreading his wings. He leaped off into a gale.

"It was just stupid," Johnson said somewhat later.

But Johnson says that with a grin and a slightly manic gleam in his eyes. You don't get the feeling he regrets it. Given the right mood and the right moment, he might be just as stupid again. And pull it off again, too.

With his dark good looks, neatly combed brown hair, and his dark, snappy suits, Johnson can look as dapper as James Bond. He is 5-foot-8 and weighs 150 pounds at his heaviest, but seems larger because his muscles are so chiseled. In his way he can be as much of a killer as James Bond. Those internal fires burn intensely.

"Harry is a fierce competitor," said Jabs.

Johnson likes to win, but really it is mediocrity that is unacceptable to him.

Take his swimming. In 1988, Johnson could only do about two laps of a pool. For a guy hoping to excel at triathlons, this was a handicap. Jabs taught him technique, and Johnson's cardiovascular system took over.

"We're looking at a gifted human being," said Jabs. "He landed on earth that way."

Johnson might demur a trifle. After all, it took him 3:35 to complete his first marathon in 1979, an hour slower than his best. That's testimony to his work ethic. Johnson says it means there's hope for everyone. He also says this: "I'm going to break 2:30 in the marathon."

Anybody who saw Johnson run the 42.7-mile Chad Ogden Ultramarathon in Kodiak in 4 hours, 45 minutes, 32 seconds on Memorial Day, 1989, will believe that. That time was only 15 seconds off the course record set by Frank Bozanich, a national champion ultrarunner.

"I had a whole bunch of buddies going," Johnson said of why he raced. "It seemed like it would be fun."

For the first 21 miles, Johnson ran with Seethaler, who then dropped out. He cruised through the marathon split in 2:47 and felt great at 30 miles. But at 35 miles, when he decided he couldn't get the record, he stopped and walked three or four times. That was a mistake because his calculations were off. If he'd pushed, he might have broken the record.

Still, Johnson's performance, challenging what had been considered a nearly unassailable mark, left an imprint.

"I was awfully, awfully impressed with his strength," said Seethaler.

Strength. Most assuredly, going fast in the Hawaii Iron Man Triathlon is about strength — strength, commitment and will.

"The guy has done real well in everything he's touched," said Rajabian.

If anyone should know Johnson's capabilities and limits, it is Rajabian. Johnson jokes that Diane is jealous of Rajabian because of all the time the close friends spend together.

They run at lunch time, ride bicycles long distances, and they swim up to three times a week at Jewel Lake in Anchorage when the weather permits.

"He does get serious," said Rajabian. "He doesn't just go out half-assed."

Once, on a stormy day, Rajabian's training schedule called for a 100-mile bike ride. He rode his stationary turbo trainer for four hours in the garage. He said it's the most boring thing he's ever done, but he never told Johnson he did it. He was afraid Harry might think it was fun and talk him into doing it again.

In 1988, Johnson did his first Iron Man-length triathlon in Penticton, British Columbia. He finished in 10 hours, 48 minutes, then the fastest time by an Alaskan.

"He really gets revved up the night before," said Rajabian, who has traveled to numerous competitions with Johnson. He has been in a position to debunk the myth that Johnson is perpetually calm. "He just really gets bent out of shape."

Johnson's 1989 Hawaii Iron Man plan called for finishing the swim in 1:15, the bike in 5:45 and the marathon in three hours.

Before the race, Johnson dissected it. Can he swim that fast? He nodded his head. Bike that fast? Doable. Run a marathon that fast after everything else? Doable. Put them all together.

For two-thirds of the race, he was well ahead of pace. He was going to do it, break 10 hours. But then he found a new definition to his limits. It took him 3:38 to complete the marathon leg. He finished in 10:14. Almost.

"A big thing is your abiliiy to endure pain," said Johnson. "I can endure a lot of pain. I'm not sure if it's getting used to it, or if you can concentrate mentally, but you can block it out."

Coming so close to 10 hours merely proved to Johnson it can be done. It told him that if he perhaps refocused his thinking a little bit, he'd break that barrier.

"Mentally, I'm going for 9:30," he said. "I need to set my goals a little higher. I kind of have a date with that sub-10 number."

That's Harry Johnson. A boy who just wants to have fun.

5

Through the Eyes of Artists

Everyone sees the world differently. Not all of us can make others see the way we saw something. Those of us who can see and explain are blessed in a special way.

Artists are among those who have special vision and their talent enables them to show the rest of the world just what they saw. They make the temporary permanent. They make transitory moments linger.

Whether it is with a camera, or paint brush and easel, artists love Alaska. They are enraptured with its breathtaking scenery; they are enthralled by the stunning diversity of its wildlife.

John Pezzenti's weapon of choice is a camera. He virtually lives among the animals he photographs, makes their haunts his haunts. He becomes a creature of the woods as he tries to record their movements, to stop time for those of us who cannot be there with him.

Jon Van Zyle in his 40s, and Fred Machetanz, in his 80s, are painters of different generations.

Van Zyle is perhaps the most popular Alaskan artist of the day, giving us scenes of the Alaska wild, many created from the first-hand adventures he's had in the Iditarod Trail Sled Dog Race.

Machetanz is the elder statesman of Alaskan artists, who has painted for more than half a century and whose work is so respected and so revered that it can no longer be obtained for less than thousands of dollars. Many of his most famous works are of polar bears on the far northern ice.

John Pezzenti
of Cooper Landing

Wildlife Photography Can Be Many Things

The grizzly bear was photogenic, but it had the same reaction to being snapped as Frank Sinatra on a bad day. It wanted to punch the photographer.

John Pezzenti approached to within 30 feet of the bear to click a picture of it standing on its hind legs, scratching its back on a wooden sign at Denali National Park that read, "Beware of Grizzly."

The bear dropped to all fours, took two bounds and slammed its head into Pezzenti, cracking four ribs.

"He knocked me 15 feet into the bushes," says Pezzenti. "It was like lightning. The picture, by the way, is entitled, 'One in a million.'"

The bear was not penalized for an illegal body check.

Pezzenti, who lives with his wife Jennifer in the Kenai Lake Lodge they operate in Cooper Landing, the tiny strip of a community on Alaska's Kenai Peninsula, shoots Alaska wildlife photographs.

He shoots startlingly vivid pictures of bears, bald eagles, moose, foxes, dall sheep, caribou, owls, and other creatures of the forest, mountains, and tundra. He has shot pictures in Denali National Park, home to Mount McKinley, about 60 times.

His work is a spectacular collection of closeups, illustrating the mood and personality of his subjects, a testimony to both his extraordinary patience to wait for the perfect moment and the ability to capture it. It takes a lot of crouching, silent moving, and most definitely long periods of waiting, to seize a brief moment. Often those waits can take place in cold, rainy, or snowy weather. It's tough on the knees and other joints. Once, Pezzenti hung by ropes from cliffs 400 feet high to get the shot of baby golden eagles.

Another example of Pezzenti's patience and dedication: a picture of the Homer Spit, with a moonrise backdrop.

"That took me a year to get," says Pezzenti.

Every time there was a full moon, Pezzenti traveled the 125 or so miles to Homer from Cooper Landing and put out into the bay in a boat. Finally, he got his picture.

Where does such patience come from?

"The beauty of what I'm watching," says Pezzenti, who has a love affair with Alaska. "I have seen so many things with my eyes, it's incredible."

Sometimes waiting around can provide amusement, and wildlife education. Pezzenti followed an enormous bull moose, with a rack of nearly 70 inches, for a long while, always in awe of its tremendous size. In the two weeks Pezzenti watched the animal, he learned that this moose was the king of the jungle. Or at least the leader of the pack.

"He had 14 females, this moose," says Pezzenti. "You know what it's like trying to get near a bull moose when he's trying to service 14 females?"

Well, you don't want to reach him at an awkward time, or he'll take his temper out on you. Moose can be benign but they are formidable beasts which can weigh over 1,000 pounds and when they are out of sorts they frequently stomp anything they can catch.

Eagles are a special passion of Pezzenti's. He has observed them and photographed them for years. A stern, imperial-like eagle, one that certainly looks as if it could be the boss of the country, was a gift to former president Ronald Reagan and the letter of appreciation from the White House hangs on the wall in Pezzenti's lodge.

Pezzenti also has a soft spot for female moose. Some might consider them to be less than beauties, but Pezzenti is infatuated and sees specialness in their seeming awkwardness. One of his favorite pictures is a very close facial shot of a female moose grazing in colorful brush.

Part of what he enjoys about shooting these moose is the challenge, he says. Moose are so plentiful in Alaska they can routinely be seen by the side of the road, so the public can grow jaded and take pictures of them for granted.

"You've got to really work to put them in a setting that's different," says Pezzenti. "Everyone thinks of them as gawky and they're really feminine beyond belief."

Viewing Pezzenti's photographs, on display at various times in such locations as the Anchorage Clarion Hotel, the Alaska Sportsman's Show, in Alaskan galleries, and in his own lodge, you can gaze deep into the brown eyes of a bear that looks as if it has just been awakened from its six-month nap and feel the anger pulsating. Pezzenti felt it. The bear charged him—one of 37 times he says he's been charged by bears in 4,000 hours of fieldwork with them—and clawed his leg after he dived under his truck.

Pezzenti says representatives of "That's Incredible" once contacted him to be on the TV show when they heard about someone who had survived all those charges, but he says he declined the offer.

"I've been in the woods my whole life," he says. "It's scary when it happens. You know when you're treading on sacred ground."

Long lenses and sophisticated equipment permit the professional photographer to get his pictures of wildlife in natural habitat without intruding. Other wildlife, notably birds, may get just as angry if someone accidentally violates their territory, but at least it's a little bit safer to have a bird ticked off.

Pezzenti felt he had to earn the trust of the Arctic terns he wished to photograph and learned that they can react to man's presence in much the same manner as bears.

"The first day, you go out and the terns attack you and crap on you and scream," says Pezzenti. "The second day, not as much. Two weeks later, they don't even know you're there."

The photographer as part of the landscape. That's the ideal situation.

"How do you like my loon?" asks Pezzenti at one point, gesturing to a photo of a loon slapping the water with her feet. Pezzenti says she is calling her babies. "She took me two and a half months."

Pezzenti looks like a man of action, somewhat stocky, with thick, dark hair and a thick mustache, and he approaches his task of shooting pictures of game and fowl much like a hunter shooting bullets. They are both stalkers, but Pezzenti doesn't surge into swift motion when he spies an animal. Instead, he settles down to study it, almost scientifically, often for long periods of time.

A biography sheet says that Pezzenti has spent 22,000 field hours in "very rural" Alaska, 6,000 with the American bald eagle alone. Actually, those numbers need updating. Add unknown extra hours to those figures.

He says he has spent close to 20 years clicking his camera, but only a few years ago did he feel ready to "go public." Since then, his work has been for sale in several Anchorage galleries and is the signature for station identification for KIMO, Channel 13 in Anchorage, the Alaska Television Network.

I knew I was always going to go public," says Pezzenti, who grew up in the very developed city of Hartford, Connecticut, but was a backpacker from his early teens.

Alaska is the Super Bowl playing field for wildlife photographers and there are many outstanding ones. Pezzenti's eye for detail and capability to capture stirring motion make him one of the best. Pezzenti describes his oneness with the wilderness and its inhabitants as lovingly and gently as a father discussing the birth of a newborn that he had helped deliver.

"I want to show the perfection of the wilderness to people," he says. "I spend two weeks in the woods with my animals before I take my cameras out, being with them, letting them know I'm one of them."

It sounds not unlike the relationship built between the researcher and the wolves in Farley Mowatt's story *Never Cry Wolf.*

Perhaps, after a while, some of the animals do get used to Pezzenti, and develop a trust for him in an oblique way — if only to recognize that he isn't there to hurt them.

"It takes hours of patience," says Pezzenti.

And the hours pay dividends. He has seen six bald eagles entangle in the sky and plummet into the water. He has watched a bull caribou fight off challenges to his authority for four days, then walk away to die in dignity, two steps after Pezzenti shot its picture.

This is not garden variety patience, but something which dwarfs waiting in line for a new Indiana Jones movie on opening night. And it is of almost monomaniacal focus. Pezzenti generally tracks one species at a time. In recent years he has pursued the Arctic tern, the loons, and the eagle.

Giving a slide show of his photos in his lodge, Pezzenti is a proud papa. As each spellbinding picture is flashed on the screen, he provides running commentary.

Of a photo of an eagle reacting to being radio collared, Pezzenti says, "This is one pissed-off bird." The picture is so sharp, the viewer can count the hairs on the bird's neck. That's detail.

Roaming through the Kenai National Wildlife Refuge, Pezzenti found his terns. A tiny baby is being fed a worm by its mother, its beak yawning open for the nourishment.

"I can get 40 feet away," says Pezzenti.

The great byproduct of watching birds is this: no more bear assaults.

"I stopped doing bears," says Pezzenti, "after I started dreaming about them."

Jon Van Zyle
of Eagle River

Artist's Brush with Iditarod Fuels Vision

The musher stood on his runners as the sled hissed across the snow and the beauty of a frozen lake. He was alone in the cold on the Iditarod Trail between Skwentna and Rainy Pass with the huge looming moon shining so brightly it illuminated the night.

The dogs galloped and the emotion swelled up in the musher's heart and at last he yelled out to the wilderness, "This is what it's all about!"

The man was in love with Alaska, in love with the moment, in love with his dogs, and in love with his experience racing the Iditarod Trail Sled Dog Race.

The man was Jon Van Zyle. The time was 1976. And if it was true that day, it is far truer today. The moment lives on as brightly as that moon in his mind, in the brush of Van Zyle. He paints it still; he paints it over and over again.

Much of the way the world sees and understands the Iditarod is seen through the eyes of Jon Van Zyle, the Eagle River artist who sees in ways we wish we could, who transports people to places, to times, in ways they could only imagine — but not as vividly as he does.

Alaskans retain images of dogs racing into the night, either because they are told stories by Rick Swenson, Susan Butcher and the other top mushers, because they see some brief television image, or by sitting and dwelling on the artistic images created by Van Zyle.

Van Zyle is the official Iditarod artist and his posters of the race have appeared annually since 1977. And that is the thing about them: they are as real to Alaskans as those real live mushers who are seen and heard; are as real to Alaskans as those real live pictures that are transmitted.

There is a reason for that. As much as Jon Van Zyle hungered and nurtured his art as he was growing up, maturing, and finally prospering, he was equally devoted to dogs. First, it was the working collies his mother raised. Then, in upstate New York, it was huskies, six of them, living in the backyard, behind the studio, and just around the corner from the jeep wagon in the driveway which has "VZ Art" Alaska license plates.

"I'll never not have them," says Van Zyle of his dogs. "It would be hard not to mix dog food at night."

Mixing dog food and mixing paints.

Van Zyle knows dogs as well as he knows brush and oil and no one has been able to capture the essence and spirit of the Iditarod, of the daunting task of racing a team of dogs 1,100 miles across Alaska from Anchorage to Nome, in any medium, as has Van Zyle.

It is, no doubt, because his love of the event, love of the basic act of mushing dogs, shares a corner of his soul with his art. His identification with the mushers is a powerful one. Once a sprint dog musher, Van Zyle found a niche in the Iditarod. Going long and steady suited him more than the stopping and starting of sprint dog training. Since those ancient days, Van Zyle has raced the Iditarod twice, in 1976 and 1979. He finished 33rd the first time and 42nd the second time.

There was something special about huskies to Jon Van Zyle. He admired the same trait that men have long admired about the breed, their toughness and commitment to hard work. Perhaps he saw his own hard work reflected back.

"I really think you have to work at what you do," says Van Zyle. "Continuously. If you get it easily, after a couple of years, it doesn't mean as much. There's something neat about a working animal. There's a lot more there. An honest dog is the type you never have to look at or worry about. That dog will work as hard as it can all the time."

People go through changes when they go through challenges. They find out how they respond when the pressure is on. They find out if they've got what it takes. Climbing a tall mountain can be such a challenge. Doing the Iditarod can be such a challenge. It was that type of transcendental experience for Van Zyle the first time he mushed the Iditarod.

"It was everything that I wanted it to be," says Van Zyle. "Basically, it completely changed my life. You find out a lot about yourself."

Somewhere on the trail, in the heart of Alaska, but in the middle of nowhere, Van Zyle did learn something about himself. He learned he had the confidence, the ability, the specialness, to do what he had dreamed of doing as an artist. And somewhere in the middle of his journey, he acquired the visions in his head that have translated so graphically—and successfully, to canvas.

"He came out of that with a vast wealth of mental images," says Dennis Corrington, Van Zyle's best friend.

Corrington, a businessman who now splits his time between Skagway, Alaska, in the summer and Missouri in the winter, also did the 1976 Iditarod, finishing nine seconds behind Van Zyle in 34th place. The two men mushed the second half of the race together. They hadn't intended to, but took turns passing each other and eventually decided what the heck, let's travel together. A friendship was born.

Van Zyle is not exaggerating when he said doing the Iditarod changed his life. Corrington saw it, too.

"It gave him the ability to know he could live with his decisions, that they were good," says Corrington. "Once you run the Iditarod, it's an affirmation you can do anything you want to do if you want to do it badly enough."

What Van Zyle wanted to do badly enough was to paint for a living. At the time, Van Zyle worked as a sales manager for Sears in Anchorage, creating 200 paintings a year and also training a dog team. Speaking of hard work and honest labor.

After the 1976 Iditarod, Van Zyle, who has a twin brother who is a successful artist in Hawaii, devoted himself to being a full-time artist, an artist who speaks loudly and eloquently of Alaska, to both Alaskans and people Outside who buy Van Zyle instead of visiting Alaska, or who buy Van Zyle as a souvenir of Alaska.

"I paint a memory and a thought," says Van Zyle.

And he so wanted it to be true to the reality of the experience. Sitting in the living room of his home 15 miles from downtown Anchorage, and surrounded by framed copies of his prints and posters, Van Zyle says, "There's nothing in there that's fake. You may make it a little bit worse or a little bet better than what actually happened."

Plenty happened. He had two leaders fall into a hole and he rescued them. He mushed past packs of wolves. He and Corrington camped out at 55 below. They stopped in villages together and visited with local Eskimo leaders. They shared stories and shared adventures. The Van Zyle that Corrington first met was a good listener.

"He is one of the most sensitive people in Alaska and it shows in his work," says Corrington.

Both men thrive in the wee hours of the morning and Van Zyle often paints in the middle of the night. Corrington says he used to get post-midnight calls from Van Zyle seeking confirmation of the accuracy of his memory.

"He would call and say, 'Dennis, if you were at Cape Nome and it was dark and we were over here, where would the moon be?' " says Corrington. "I'd say, 'What time is it?' And we'd go from there."

V an Zyle is bald, has a gray and white beard, wire rim glasses, and a slightly expanding girth. He is a soft-spoken man who considers his words carefully when expressing his thoughts and can grow misty-eyed when discussing his own deep emotional attachment to the Iditarod and his experiences in it.

"A feeling is more what I try to paint," he says. "I never painted anything I've never physically done. The measure of my success is that what I'm doing is getting across to people. Somewhere in there I am expressing feelings. I'm not the best painter in the world."

He is certainly one of the best in Alaska, and one of the most successful. Currently, the 30 to 40 originals Van Zyle paints annually sell for several thousand dollars each. His half-dozen new prints a year sell for hundreds of dollars each and his four new posters a year sell for $25 each. Something in every price range. Distribution is taken care of through Alaska Limited Editions, His wife Charlotte's company. And the newest and a comparatively inexpensive way to obtain a Van Zyle is to buy a book of his collected art entitled *Best of Alaska: The Art of Jon Van Zyle*.

Corrington says he knew years ago that Van Zyle had the talent to become something special.

"I didn't have any doubts about it," says Corrington. "If he had good luck. I knew where he was and he would continue to grow."

Becoming the official Iditarod artist at a time the race captured the fancy of the state was the break Van Zyle needed. He was the right man in the right place, with the right talent.

"That was a real nice honor for me," says Van Zyle. "And it may not mean the same thing to someone else as it does to me."

Of course, not all of Van Zyle's paintings are of dogs, or are Iditarod-related. Many are of mountains, of fishing scenes, of wolves howling at the moon, of loons, of snow-covered wilderness cabins with smoke pouring from the chimney. There's even one of his good buddy Corrington.

There are pictures of haunting, weathered faces, or knowing eyes, hovering ghost-like and protective above children or campsites. There are pictures of foxes, birds, and grizzly bears, in their habitat.

There is a definitive Van Zyle style, once seen, always recognized. His colors are only rarely bright; usually they are the hues of the territory, often of scenes at night. They are blacks and whites, crisp, but not brilliant or flashy, and magical deep blues are often dominant.

Van Zyle is a chronicler of the Alaskan way of life and he is pleased to be able to stop time in his manner.

"I guess I'm fortunate I live here," says Van Zyle, who is nearing 50. As a youth he lived in upstate New York and in Colorado.

"If I were painting Connecticut, I don't know if it would have the same appeal. I still paint only Alaska. There's a national or international acceptance of that work because it transcends borders. I know there's something about this state. The mystique is so tremendous."

Van Zyle knows he is touching a chord of romanticism both in Alaskans who love their home state and people Outside who have seen his work in museums and galleries all up and down the West Coast.

"Very definitely," he says.

The mystique of the Iditarod has lingered within Van Zyle. He mustered the resources to do the race a second time in 1979, but has never done it again and doubts that he will. Not because he doesn't want to, but at least partially because he broke a kneecap and that would hinder him. The knee has never been 100 percent again.

He also probably won't race the big one again partially because he is who he is now. It takes so much time to train a team of dogs to compete in such a demanding event that a popular artist with obligations to himself to make a living, and to a public which seeks his work, can't find enough hours in the day to do both.

"If you can't do something 100 percent, then why try to do it at all?" Van Zyle asks.

Van Zyle is 100 percent artist these days, with originals on display in museums and posters available in galleries and some bookstores. Success sometimes makes artists aloof. Sometimes they grow so big they don't like to mingle with the masses; but Van Zyle says he genuinely enjoys the autograph session he does in shopping malls in Anchorage.

He is an engaging fellow at these events, taking time to chat with those who purchase his posters and book, taking time to ask their names and even to ask what they like to do. Then, not only does he sign his name, he usually draws a picture for them as well.

It takes a patient man to do that because when Van Zyle appears in public the line wraps its way through aisleways and out the door of the store or the door of the mall.

"These are the people who made you what you are," he says. "You can't ignore them. That's one of the reasons I started doing posters. More people can afford them. Growing up, we had very little money; but art—you should be able to have it. Some of the most satisfying things I do for people is poster signings. It's that one communication that I really like that tells you people care."

He also stays in touch with the people and Alaska in other ways. Following the *Exxon Valdez* oil spill in Prince William Sound, Van Zyle painted a picture he called "Hushed Sound." The proceeds from its sale were donated to a bird treatment center. He keeps few originals, actually.

"Part of why we do it," he says of artists, "is maybe looking for acceptance and maybe wanting to tell a story. If we were to just do it and not have it appreciated by people in some manner, shape, or form, then we'd be cheating the people. We are given these talents to communicate. If you're doing something and leaving it in the closet, then you're only making one person happy.

"I'm one of the luckiest people in the world because I live here and I can live here by what I do here. I do it 14 to 16 hours a day when I paint. It's your own thing and you love it. I'll just paint forever."

Van Zyle often thinks of his first Iditarod. When he reached Nome at the end of his 1976 race, he was not emotionally spent, he was emotionally high.

"It was like I wanted to keep on going," says Van Zyle, "to keep on going to Teller, then to Wales."

It is easy to see that Van Zyle actually did keep on going. All of those Iditarod scenes, the dog racing scenes, Van Zyle has painted were his way of keeping on that trail. Jon Van Zyle is yet mushing across Alaska.

Fred Machetanz
of Palmer

Polar Bears and Men of the Arctic Ice

Those who know the work of Fred Machetanz, the preeminent living Alaskan artist, love his scenes of the Arctic, of Eskimos in their boats hunting seal, of the mysterious blues that pervade the ice, of polar bears hunting and at play. Especially his polar bears.

Of all the colorful and evocative scenes the octogenarian painter has produced, none have been more closely identified with him than the many paintings of polar bears. Yet polar bears seem as if they could leap out of Machetanz' paintings and take a swat at you.

And yet, unbelievably, Machetanz, Alaskan adventurer, Alaskan resident for nearly a half century, has never seen a polar bear in the wild.

"I never did see one," said Machetanz.

But he has seen everything else. He has lived among natives of Alaska in Unalakleet by the Bering Sea coast and recorded their way of life. He has seen trappers in the wilderness and recorded their way of life. Old-timers and huskies; he's recorded their habits, as well.

There are no automobiles or highrise buildings in the 500 or so paintings Machetanz—perhaps Alaska's most famed and beloved artist since Sydney Laurence's death in 1940—has produced in the past 35 years. No, he captures a way of life in the Great Land that was a way of life long ago. The vision of Alaska Machetanz preserves is the way the land was when he was younger, the way it was before the state was a state and before it became so grownup as to become an international air crossroads.

"The Alaska I paint is the prewar Alaska," said Machetanz, who was born in 1908 in Ohio and came to Alaska at the invitation of his uncle, Charles Traeger, in 1935. Traeger offered a free six-week vacation. Machetanz stayed for two years. He kept coming back, then moved to Palmer, 50 miles north of Anchorage, in 1950.

Machetanz, a slender, white-haired man with thick, bushy eyebrows and glasses that dangle from a string around his neck, is unlikely to utter an expression more vehement than "good night," as an exclamation of amazement or anger. Not that he would say anything truly nasty about progress anyway.

"It's certainly more pleasant to drive to Anchorage on a highway than a mud-covered road," he said. "The niceties of civilization, I would miss that now."

Machetanz didn't miss them back in the 1930s, however, when Alaska, which now has about 500,000 people, had less than 70,000 residents. Those people shared a kindred spirit being in the north and Machetanz believes the place was different then.

"It was friendlier," he said. "It was said, whether true or not, that people never locked their cabin doors. It's not true anymore."

It is clear both from chatting with Machetanz in the airy room that serves as both living room and studio in his log home tucked in the trees comfortably away from too much civilization, that it is the romance of Alaska which captured his mind and soul when he was young, the romance of Alaska which has endured, and the romance of Alaska he seeks to capture in his painting.

It works.

In 1981, *American Artist* magazine selected Machetanz as its artist of the year and commissioned him to produce a painting for its American Artists Collection. The magazine described Machetanz as "a national treasure."

The national treasure was born in Kenyon, Ohio, and first became entranced by drawing at the age of 11.

"I saw some pen sketches in the Sunday paper and I tried to copy them," said Machetanz.

A year later, Machetanz saw some paintings by artist Maxfield Parrish, wrote him a fan letter, and got an autograph.

Parrish, who painted many sunlit landscapes, was an early influence. Much later, Machetanz borrowed his aunt's 1917 Ford and drove east with a friend to visit Parrish unannounced in New Hampshire. The car nearly died on a huge hill in West Virginia and it took some hood-up repairs by Machetanz to make it. Parrish received him warmly.

"He was a wonderful inspiration," said Machetanz of the artist who died at age 94 in 1964. "It was just fascinating to be around him."

Machetanz became an art student at Ohio State, where he was also a 125-pound quarterback for the football team and a competitor on the track team. There he learned from Will Rannels and James Hopkins.

Those two men, plus Parrish, "were the three key people in my beginnings," said Machetanz.

He eventually earned Bachelor of Arts and Master of Fine Arts degrees from Ohio State and, later, studied at the Chicago Art Institute.

Machetanz didn't have many heroic moments on the gridiron, but for 13 years from the late 1920s to the early 1940s, he created the covers for Buckeye football game programs. His love of football endured, too, and over six decades later, Machetanz proudly wears a jacket to Palmer High football games proclaiming him the "No. 1 Fan."

That team also plays its home games at Machetanz Field.

Actually, when he first enrolled at Ohio State, Machetanz thought he might become a lawyer. Friends and relatives tried to discourage him from switching to art.

"They said, 'Fred, don't do it. There's no money in it,'" he said. "'Be a lawyer and be a success.'"

None of them ever dreamed he would be able to speak more eloquently with a paint brush than in summing up cases for a jury.

The turning point in Machetanz's life was the trip to Alaska offered by his uncle, who had moved here in 1898 in pursuit of gold and who had opened a trading post in the Eskimo village of Unalakleet when he failed to find riches.

Even while sailing the inside passage through southeastern Alaska before reaching his destination, Machetanz made the decision that he must come to live in this beautiful place.

"That was the first time a boy from Ohio saw mountains and glaciers," said Machetanz.

"I don't fish and I don't hunt, but the other qualities of Alaska appealed to me, the scenery, the mountains, the landscapes, and the people. And living among the Eskimos with my uncle, I did sketching and gained a lot of material from my stay.

"I never thought I would like Alaska that much. I was never interested in the outdoors or camping."

A little later, Machetanz was able to ride on a Coast Guard ship as it patrolled the Arctic waters. This had its good points — he was able to visit many otherwise inaccessible villages — and its bad points.

"I realized I was susceptible to seasickness," he said dryly.

When World War II began, Machetanz requested duty in Alaska, was assigned to the Aleutian Islands — and saw another whole region of the territory.

"I've really been practically over every part of Alaska," he said.

Machetanz's artistic breakthrough was partly attributable to the good fortune he had in penetrating the local society of Unalakleet. Typically, the Natives would not so readily accept a visiting white man; but a strange incident occurred when Machetanz arrived. The village chief's wife almost fainted when she saw him because he so resembled a son of hers who had died. She thought for a moment the son had come back to life.

"She gave me an entree to the villagers more than my uncle could," said Machetanz.

Following the first two-year stint in Alaska, Machetanz approached publishers hoping to sell his illustrations for use with some book about Alaska. Machetanz was told if he wanted to illustrate a book about the region, he'd have to write it himself. He did. He wrote two, in fact, *Panuk, Eskimo Sled Dog,* was published in 1939 and *On Arctic Ice* was published in 1940.

It should be no surprise that Machetanz attaches romantic notions to Alaska. After all, he fell in love there. After the war, he returned to Alaska and met Sara Dunn. He saw her at an autograph party.

"But she didn't notice me and I thought, 'Well, ships that pass in the night,' " said Machetanz.

However, when Machetanz continued his journey by ship, heading to Skagway and the Yukon Territory, Sara was on board. He chatted with her a bit and then, before docking, he casually hinted in as loud a voice as he politely could that there was only one place to stay in Skagway.

Machetanz went to that place and waited. And waited. Many hours later he looked out the window and there was Sara coming up the walk with a suitcase. That afternoon they went hiking and took pictures and when Machetanz left for the Yukon, Sara went with him. And stayed with him. They got married in Unalakleet in January, 1947. Machetanz hurried the process along by telling her that they had to get married within three days because the missionary was leaving, even though he wasn't planning to depart until spring.

"Our honeymoon was by dog team to St. Michael's," said Machetanz.

That's a tiny village 60 miles away on the western Arctic coast of Alaska.

When Mrs. Manchetanz sent a picture home to her parents in Tennessee to show off her new husband, she got a reply reading, "Needless to say, we're deeply shocked."

They were repelled by Machetanz's thick beard. The beard was a bit of help on minus-50-degree days, though the real reason he grew it was a temporary sensitivity from a frostbitten face. Some of that frostbite damage was on his nose and 50 years later the white spot is still visible.

The Machetanz's partnership was professional as well as romantic. They had many adventures in the wild together. Once, Fred had the chance to go on a whale hunt, but one of the incidents Sara recalls best wasn't even particularly germane to the local surroundings.

"A bush plane just about terminated his entire career," said Mrs. Machetanz.

Machetanz was in the plane as a passenger when the pilot got the propeller going. However, the plane started to roll away on the ice toward the Bering Sea. Machetanz didn't know how to fly.

"I had enough brains to know where the ignition key was and to turn it off," said Machetanz.

Fred and Sara Machetanz collaborated on eight books about Alaska and made documentary films. And for parts of the first 15 years of their marriage, they gave lectures in the lower 48 states.

"I wasn't able to make a living through my art," said Machetanz.

That changed dramatically on one astounding day. Several well-off and influential Anchorage businessmen who were friends of Machetanz urged him to spend more time painting. He told them he couldn't because he needed to eat. They responded by financing his living expenses in 1961.

The Fred Machetanz one-man show that followed at the Westward Hotel in Anchorage in 1962 was a spectacular success.

"At the opening of that exhibit, I broke out in hives," said Machetanz.

Who could blame him for being a trifle worried? He was in his 50s and his dream would either at long last be realized or be shattered.

There was no reason to worry, after all. Machetanz abruptly went from virtual unknown to shooting star. There were 44 paintings in the show and 24 of them sold in 15 hours. He grossed $10,000 and although single Machetanz paintings sell for double that amount now, it seemed like a very large sum of money to him then.

"It was something I'd never had, ever," he said. "That was my coming out party."

How did the money change their lives?

"We started paying income tax for the first time," said Mrs. Machetanz.

They've been paying ever since. Gladly.

Even though Machetanz has never encountered a polar bear in the wild, his wife and son Traeger have. They were having lunch on the shore of the Arctic Ocean in Point Barrow and watched from a distance as a hunter seeking dinner was being stalked by a polar bear from behind.

"It was like it was staged for their benefit," said Machetanz.

So many of Machetanz's popular works involve polar bears — "Mighty Hunter," "Spring Fever," "The Tender Arctic" among them — that it is truly mind-boggling to realize he has seen the huge, white-haired beasts only up close in zoos. He studies them there.

"You can't see polar bears in the wild very well," said Machetanz.

Once, at the Memphis Zoo, Sara was wearing a seal parka. The polar bears were asleep. But when she approached their cage, they began to stir. They woke up, moved to the edge of the pit and sniffed the air.

Their reaction, said Fred, was "Oh, that's just a coincidence. They couldn't smell it after it's been tanned."

Then the same thing happened at the St. Louis Zoo. Those polar bears impressed Machetanz plenty in captivity.

"You think of polar bears as a nice, cuddly thing to be around," he said, "but they say they are as vicious an animal as known to man."

There are stories behind many of the paintings Machetanz has done and many of them are modeled on real people, including the Natives of Unalakleet and other Alaskan sourdoughs. One painting, still hanging in Machetanz's living room, is of a trapper with a thickly flowing beard. The annual Anchorage Fur Rendezvous carnival had a contest for the best beard and that man had won it, said Machetanz. But he did not keep it for good.

"His wife was dying," said Machetanz, "and she made the request that he should shave so she could remember him how he looked long ago. He never grew it back."

Machetanz's popularity grew in such spurts that the line for his commissions became so long he fell years behind. Some 15 years ago he took on many assignments at a fixed price of $1,900 for a large painting and $200 for a smaller one. In the winter of 1990 he was just fulfilling the final order and even though those $1,900 paintings are now valued at $10,000, he was planning to sell it for $1,900.

"That was the price we agreed on," said Machetanz.

Machetanz still paints a dozen or more paintings a year and just about all of them are for sale. All except a portrait of Traeger and one of Machetanz's favorite huskies, Seego, from decades ago. Those will stay in the family.

"Those two we couldn't part with," said Machetanz. "The rest I like to have purchased. It makes me feel good that someone looks at my work and it supposedly gives them pleasure."

From the first moments he laid eyes on the country and felt it was the place he was destined to paint, Machetanz has appreciated Alaska. He and his wife feel strongly that Alaskans appreciate Alaskan art.

"In the past, (Alaska) being smaller in population, the residents got to know the artists better," said Mrs.

Machetanz. "They would have a personal feeling about the art and it was a form of art everybody could have."

"The artists painted so much of the country and what they knew. It was decorative to have a little color in the house for the long winter days."

It must be still because Alaskans have never tired of Fred Machetanz's art. And he has never tired of giving them what he feels they want: his vision of Alaska's beauty.

"I still feel there is more original artwork in Alaskan homes than anywhere else in the United States. There are so many darned good subjects," he said. "The mountains, the sourdoughs. There was a romance to the country."

That romance lives on for sure in the hand of Fred Machetanz.

6

Real Alaskans

There are some Alaskans who just seem to be part of the landscape. They have distinguished themselves in a special way and they have become legends for that special thing.

Where there's action and danger in the air, that's where you'll find pilot Jim Okonek. Not that he specifically seeks it. On the contrary, people are forever calling him to get them out of trouble. He doesn't seem able to refuse them.

Reggie Joule is a hero to his people, the Natives of Alaska, who settled the Great Land first. He is a hero because he has been a leader in preserving culture, in living a lifestyle that speaks of pride in the Eskimo way of life.

Perhaps more than any other sporting or outdoors figure in Alaska, George Attla is a household name. There was a time when Attla was merely a sports star for his sprint mushing, famous within his sport. Then came a time when he was both sports star and famous beyond his sport. Now, simply, Attla is a legend.

He has endured and been triumphant for so long that he has become as much a part of the state's history and identification as Mount McKinley itself. Attla is not only of the past, he is of the present. And as he promises us, of the future, as well. There is no one like him.

Jim Okonek
of Talkeetna

Pilot Turns Saving Lives into a Career

The chopper flew low, skimming the treetops, but the bullets traced a row of dots down its side and ripped into the cockpit.

Blades cutting the air, the helicopter tilted, but it flew. Day after day, crisscrossing the Mekong Delta, Jim Okonek flew, plucking wounded, bloodied American servicemen off the ground, off boats on rivers, as Viet Cong huddled in rice paddies unleashed thousands of rounds of machine-gun bullets. The bullets whizzed past his head—but they never hit him.

"I don't remember being particularly frightened," said Okonek. "Later on, you'd lose a lot of sleep. You'd lay awake reliving the whole thing over and over."

Much of the year that Okonek spent in Vietnam, during part of 1967 and in 1968 during and after the Tet Offensive, was like that: under fire.

But these days, most of the runs that Okonek makes as a pilot are much more sedate. As owner of K-2 Aviation in the cozy town of Talkeetna 110 miles north of Anchorage, he is best known for flying climbers to Mount McKinley and other peaks in the Alaska Range — and tourists around picturesque glaciers.

Spend an hour in the air. I'll show you Alaska. That's the core of Okonek's business. Tourists generally don't want to dodge bullets and most of the clients will never hear the war stories. Meeting Okonek, they probably wouldn't ever suspect he's led anything but a calm existence.

Okonek, who is in his late 50s, is a slow-talking, unexcitable man given to wearing work shirts, blue jeans, and baseball caps. It is an image which belies the James Bond-caliber danger he has faced and shrugged off over the past 35 years.

"He's always kept the whole family truly entertained at the dinner table," said son Brian Okonek, a mountaineering guide. "Every night at the dinner table, it was a different story."

Jim Okonek has spent a lifetime saving lives — uncounted hundreds of them — rescuing people in distress, whether they were on high snow-coated mountains, stranded in bushwhack-thick terrain, stuck on a roof during a flood, or flailing helplessly in a churning sea. He's done it in helicopters and small planes, done it in Vietnam, Texas, California, and Alaska.

The people facing desperate moments might be panicking, but Okonek never did. The more than 20 medals he's been awarded testify to that.

Not only can Okonek land on a dime, he can pick it up. The Air Force taught him how and eventually made him into a Lieutenant Colonel.

Okonek grew up in Wisconsin and went to Superior State College, mostly because he didn't know what else to do with himself. But by 1952, in his second school year, wondering about the right thing to do with his life, he was thinking jets. As a kid he'd wanted to be a cowboy, an FBI agent, or a pilot. The pilot thought itched more and itched longer, primarily because it seemed to be a glamorous lifestyle and, though he admits it might have been an immature outlook, it was nonetheless a real desire and did present a path to follow to a career.

"I felt the opportunity was passing me by," said Okonek, leaning back in a chair in his office at the Talkeetna Airport. "I trained in fighters and the war was over."

That war was the Korean War and Okonek was trained to fly fighters just in time not to be needed. The United States was reducing its forces and if a young man wanted to stay in the military he needed a different kind of skill. Okonek shifted to helicopter training, became a specialist, and stayed in the Air Force for 21 years.

Helicopter flying was in its infancy. There were no millionaires landing themselves on the roofs of skyscrapers in the early 1950s. People were only just beginning to understand the maneuverability of the small craft. Okonek was lucky enough to fly as he wanted—and he did get a belated visit to Korea.

Stationed near the DMZ after the truce between North and South Korea, Okonek was called on to retrieve a downed U.S. Navy pilot across the border. He had an uninterrupted flight to the wreckage, but as he circled, ground fire erupted. It was a trap.

"They let us come right on in and started shooting," said Okonek.

He never found the pilot and the U.S. had to explain his presence over North Korean soil as pilot error.

Until Vietnam, Okonek's rescues did not routinely occur with people shooting at him. But they were far from routine occurrences. Being an expert helicopter pilot in California during the 1950s meant you were a busy guy.

"We stood like firemen on alert waiting on a call," said Okonek. "We were out the door in a finger snap."

Okonek was stationed near Edwards Air Force Base — where the test pilots challenged themselves to see if they had the right stuff and to see if their planes could break the sound barrier. They had a lot of gumption, but they also had a lot of problems.

"They were dropping out of the sky like flies," said Okonek. "There were a lot of accidents. I thought for a while it was just routine that a unit lost a plane a week."

One pilot bailed out in the hills near Los Angeles. The rescue was complicated by one of those raging California drought blazes and when Okonek arrived on the scene he had to play the fire, the wind, the smoke, and the visibility, and dodge the heat. He got his man. And got a medal for it.

Another time, when he was stationed in Texas, Okonek responded to a flash flood on a branch of the Red River near the Texas-Oklahoma border. People were stuck on the roofs of buildings and some had climbed trees to escape the fast-rising water.

Okonek hovered above them in his tiny Bell two-seater helicopter and lowered a hoist carefully. The trick in a tree rescue was to avoid entanglement in a limb.

"The strange thing I remember was that you had the sensation you were moving when you were trying to maintain a stationary hover because the water was flowing beneath them," said Okonek.

Okonek may leave a listener wide-eyed as he relates his tales, but even though he might say that such and such a rescue was exciting, or even scary, his tone of his voice is as matter-of-fact as a daddy telling a bedtime story.

It is not as if Okonek, who wears tinted glasses and who now has a mix of gray and white hair and a weathered face, isn't proud of what he did. It's just that performing rescues requires the temperament of a judge making considered decisions, rather than the irritability of a basketball coach screaming at referees.

"You're expected to do it," said Okonek. "The thing that's pretty weird is that when you're out trying to help someone, you have a tendency to push your limits and go beyond the ordinary limits of your ability or your aircraft. Policemen do. Firemen do.

"People tend to take chances because it's somebody else's only chance."

When Okonek received new orders in 1964, he thought he was on his way to Vietnam.

"Everybody I knew was going to Vietnam," said Okonek. "I expected to. I didn't really relish the idea, but I felt I ought to."

But Okonek was surprised. He was on his way to Alaska instead.

He was thrilled. Not only would he keep flying as part of the Rescue Coordination Center, which operates out of Elmendorf Air Force Base in Anchorage, but also he could hunt and fish all the time.

Okonek piled his wife Julie, baby daughter Jamie, and young son Brian into the car and headed north for what would become another series of adventures in quirky helicopter searches and rescues.

For the next nine years, with the exception of his year-long tour in Vietnam, Okonek either flew helicopter rescues or coordinated them for the military in Alaska. That meant learning the nasty ways of snow and icestorms and the geography of the vast state.

One rescue Okonek supervised in the 1960s involved a search off the coast of Nome for some scientists who had drifted off in a kayak. The search went on for days. Then the scientists were spotted a couple of miles away floating on a hunk of ice, not by the planes, but by a woman on Front Street downtown looking seaward.

"They couldn't get to shore, but they were in view of town day and night," said Okonek.

In 1967, Okonek also coordinated the rescue of the first McKinley winter ascent party which placed Art Davidson, Ray Genet, and Dave Johnston on the summit of North America's highest peak.

Okonek, the man on the walkie-talkie, received advice from prominent Alaska bush pilot Don Sheldon, and famed climbers Lou and Jim Whittaker, and others. The mountain was obscured by stormy weather and the climbers, who were overdue, hadn't been seen in days.

"We were seeing nothing of anybody," said Okonek. "The pilots would see bits and pieces of the mountain. We thought we'd never see the climbers again."

But just as a search plane flew near the top of the mountain, the men emerged from a snow cave.

"It was the first time the weather had broken," said Okonek. "The timing was perfect. Everybody was elated."

The climbers slowly and painfully descended to 13,000 feet, where they were picked up.

"They were in bad shape," said Okonek.

Bad enough shape to be hospitalized for some time. But the rescue helped provide the pioneer ascent with a happy ending. The climbers' rescue also epitomized one of the truisms of rescues in Alaska: weather is always a factor.

"Usually, the weather contributes to an accident and it delays any kind of rescue effort," said Okonek.

During Okonek's years working at the Rescue Coordination Center, there were an average of 400 cases a year.

That's more than a search a day. There wasn't time to have a case of nerves every time the alarm went off.

Okonek was 41 when he retired from the Air Force in 1973 with no concrete plans except to fish, but with a fear of not flying.

"The only thing I knew how to do was fly," he said.

He had long before turned down a chance to fly helicopters in Chicago, a shuttle between downtown and the airport.

"It was going to be a bus driver situation," said Okonek.

And it sounded boring. That wasn't a post-military job that promised satisfaction.

When he left the Air Force, Okonek bought a tiny Super Cub, taught junior ROTC at East High in Anchorage for three years, and built a cabin 18 miles from Talkeetna. He flew some for veteran pilot Cliff Hudson and flew son Brian to McKinley on request.

He even did some more helicopter rescue work and was named pilot of the year by the Helicopter Association of America for nine rescues of 12 people on McKinley and in the Alaska Range in 1980.

The most spectacular rescue Okonek has made in the high mountains of the Alaskan Interior turned out not to be a rescue but a taxi ride.

A radio signal was picked up and read to mean "Climbers in trouble on the northeast ridge of Mount Foraker." Then communications broke off. The weather was awful, snowing and blowing. But Okonek flew.

It was that sense of duty, that feeling that you, with the rescue vehicle, are someone's only chance, that propelled Okonek out the door.

"You assume there are survivors and they need assistance," said Okonek. "You go with the idea you're going to help somebody."

Coincidentally, camped beneath the mountain, on a glacier, Brian Okonek, was watching the sky, not knowing his father was in the copter overhead.

"I do remember thinking it wasn't a very good day for flying," he said. "There weren't any other helicopters out there that day."

Risking his life, Okonek made contact and found five climbers. Word came back that only three wanted to leave. Huh? It turned out the climbers were not in danger, but in a hurry.

"I had stuck my butt way out and all they wanted was a ride home," said Okonek.

When Okonek gave up helicopters and switched to small planes like the Super Cub and Cessna 185s he now owns, he wasn't sure he could handle them as well. But it turned out the skills were compatible.

Ask Roger Cowles. In 1979, Cowles, Brian Okonek and Dave Johnston made a first-route ascent of Foraker, the second-highest mountain in the Alaska Range. The ascent has endured in climbing lore for another reason. It's remembered as the time Cowles forgot his sleeping bag.

A good tale, but not strictly true.

Cowles, an Anchorage carpenter, was then living in a cabin near Talkeetna. On the morning of departure, he checked his gear and loaded it onto a sled attached to a snowmachine. Then he, his girlfriend, and dog drove to Swan Lake, the Okonek wilderness homestead.

The three climbers' equipment was dumped into one pile and in three trips hauled by Jim Okonek to Foraker. Only after Okonek flew away, with instructions from the men not to return for three weeks, did Cowles realize his bag was missing.

Then a storm blew in and trapped the men at base camp, forcing some improvisational sleeping arrangements. Cowles was frantic, wondering what he was going to do. He needed a sleeping bag to proceed with the climb.

But when the first narrow patch of blue appeared in the sky, the buzz of a plane could be heard. It was Okonek. Dipping through the clouds, he descended to an altitude of a few thousand feet. Something was hurled from the plane. It landed right in camp. Extra points for accuracy.

"I couldn't believe it," says Cowles.

It was the sleeping bag—with a note attached. It turned out the bag had bounced off the sled. Retracing their path on the way back to the cabin, Cowles's girlfriend and dog passed by the area where they had hit a bump. The dog began barking furiously. It had detected the scent of its master and it wouldn't cool off until it led the young lady to the sleeping bag. Recognizing the gravity of the situation, she promptly took it to Okonek.

Cowles, who has flown with Okonek many times, said he always feels comfortable flying with him.

"He knows aviation inside out," said Cowles. "He has so much experience. He can look at the snow and see what kind of landing it will be. I always know I'm going to be safe with Jim."

Bush pilots have a derring-do image. They are pictured flying sideways through mountain passes, flying by instinct rather than navigational aids, as being swashbucklers who have ice water in their veins and who take risks no human with a normal stomach would take.

False, insisted Okonek. A lot of people in the aviation industry like people to think flying small planes is like wrestling alligators, but Okonek often refuses to fly to McKinley in the winter. He often refuses to take what he considers to be ill-prepared soloist mountain climbers there.

"I felt it was suicidal," he said of climbers he has refused passage to.

Okonek was in the business of saving lives for so long he has no desire to place people in situations that might need rescues. No, these days, Okonek is most interested in putting people in situations where they can appreciate the beauty of Mount McKinley and its surrounding areas. Okonek has flown 6,500 hours in the Alaska Range, viewing McKinley, Foraker, Mount Deborah, and other mountains from the tiny windows of his planes.

K-2, his company, flew 3,000 people to remote areas of the state in 1989. They came from 23 different countries and 90 percent of them viewed McKinley and its 20,320-foot bulk.

"It's just so beautiful and everchanging," said Okonek. "What I enjoy about my job is showing McKinley to people. I can be enthusiastic about it day after day."

Even when it's snowing? Which it certainly does often enough around McKinley. Well . . .

"The weather is the most exasperating thing about the mountain," said Okonek. "The weather does dictate when you can go. The record is 17 days without being able to land at base camp."

The weather does make the decision to fly or not to fly and while others might say, "yeah, that's what Alaska's all about, you've got to go even if it's snowing," Jim Okonek's advice is nope, stay home when it's snowing.

"We only go when the weather is good," he said. "After all, the mail doesn't have to go through."

Reggie
Joule
of Kotzebue

How High Can His Dream Fly?

Reggie Joule drove his pickup truck over the flat, snow-covered dirt on Second Avenue in Kotzebue. Right over — or under, really — the spot where he first learned to fly some 25 years ago.

That first time his body was tossed into a bright blue Midnight Sun sky on a Fourth of July, a young, skinny 11-year-old Joule soared high enough to see the nearby water of the bay leading to the Chukchi Sea.

Exhilaration seized his heart. This was wonderful, he thought. But like Icarus he had flown too close to the sun. Fear seized his heart. He was going to miss the blanket. Joule plummeted toward the ground, plotting how he would tumble and roll and save himself.

At the last second, a strong man stepped out, caught him under the arms, and placed him gently upright on land.

"I was scared," said Joule. "I said, 'Thank you,' turned around and walked away."

Thinking never again. Only Joule accidentally walked right onto the blanket again. The crowd, invigorated by this boldness, lifted Joule and tossed him skyward once more. Joule, shock hanging his mouth open, conquered his pounding heart as he flew.

The king of the Eskimo blanket toss learned immediately that falling off the edge of the small, circular world was just like falling off a bicycle. You cannot let the hurt and worry linger. You must climb back on.

"I was able to take care of that fear right away," said Joule. "If I hadn't, I never would have done it again."

And if he hadn't, this eloquent spokesman for his people, the Inupiat Eskimo of Northern Alaska, might have been muted.

Reggie Joule is the man who has shown much of America the blanket toss, the two-foot high kick, and the other sports of Alaska Natives. He has done it on the Tonight Show with Johnny Carson, on the Today Show with Bryant Gumbel, and at the Smithsonian Institution in Washington, D.C.

Joule has taught many Americans how to fly, too. But he has taught many young Inupiat how to live. He has taught the old ways to the new generation.

The games of the World Eskimo Indian Olympics in Fairbanks and the Native Youth Olympics in Anchorage are not merely sport, but testimony to survival. Each game has roots in surviving the harsh winter climate of the Arctic. More than anywhere else in sport, it is not whether one wins or loses, but that the game is played at all.

Joule has played all the Native games and played them well. But the blanket toss remains his favorite, remains the event that still brings him the most joy, even though, at 38, he is mostly retired from competition.

He told Gumbel the toss was his favorite because all he had to do was stand on the skin and get thrown in the air. How can this be so if so many others can barely stand upright? How can this be so if no other can go so high, leap so smoothly, or come so close to touching the sky? This is Reggie Joule's modesty. He is a master, but not a braggart. There is more science to the blanket toss than letting the pullers do all the work.

Watch Joule's brown eyes as he describes the blanket toss. They grow wide with pleasure and glisten.

"It's just a real neat feeling when you're up there," said Joule. "Once you get used to it. When they made the trampoline, I think it was a refined blanket toss."

The blanket is made of the skin of the walrus or a bearded seal. Bearded seal skin is often used in the making of whaling boats. Walrus skins are more common in the St. Lawrence Island area. Joule said the walrus skin is thicker and more durable.

The blanket toss has a long history. In the villages, it is usually part of a celebration marking the killing of a whale or some other successful hunt.

Regardless of how light he may be or the spring in his legs, the tossee does need strong, capable pullers. Once at the World Eskimo Indian Olympics, when he was much younger, Joule was tossed errantly. He broke his leg and accepted the honor as the meet's outstanding athlete while sitting in a wheelchair.

"They need to keep the blanket tight at all times," said Joule. "The people need to be placed so there's equal strength all around and they have to pull together. If you watch people who have never done it before, there's a tendency to bend their arms. You use your whole body. It's a rocking motion."

The person being thrown must not bend the knees. If the pullers are true and the blanket stays taut, he can fly very high indeed. At the Big Dipper or the Patty Gym in Fairbanks during the Eskimo Indian Olympics, the crowd oohs and ahs when competitors stretch toward the mirrored ceiling, and the people explode when it is touched.

The younger Joule, at his best, could touch the ceiling, spin and do backflips. He was the Dr. J (Julius Erving) of the blanket toss. They really oohed and ahed for Reggie.

"It's like a towel whip," said Joule. "That's kind of the principle on a skin that's coming up."

Raised by his grandfather, the respected Eskimo educator Tony Joule, Reggie was a muscular and agile young man. By age 18 he was dominating the blanket toss at the Eskimo Indian Olympics. He eventually won 13 gold medals in the event. And year after year he won medals in every sport he tried.

The young boy who never learned to hunt—and keenly felt that inadequacy—had found his niche, found a way to both understand and live his heritage.

It took longer to find humility, to understand that his victories in the blanket toss, the high kicks, greased pole walk, arm pull, ear pull, and other events, meant more than pasteups for his scrapbook.

"When I got involved with Native sports it was something that made me No. 1, made me aware of my heritage and culture, and something that I was good at, even if I couldn't do the other things," said Joule.

"It gave me a sense of connectedness, of Nativeness, that really meant something to me."

Summer after summer Joule would return to Kotzebue with his medals, where, "The old folks would say, 'You make us proud,' " said Joule.

Gradually, he came to realize that yes, he got to keep the medals, but his triumphs belonged to all. The old people who shared them saw in Joule a vibrant future for their own way of life, a way of life squeezed hard between the ways of the white man and the thrusts of modernization and progress. Their nods and smiles and words told him: We live on in you.

It was cold outside and the ice had come to this community of 3,500 on the western Arctic coast by the third week in October. Joule planned to go ice fishing the next day. But inside the warm, pleasant home of the Joules, the past, present, and future mixed comfortably.

Guests shared conversation and a caribou roast with the Reggie Joule family. Reggie met Linda, his wife of 15 years, when she was runnerup for the Miss WEIO title in 1972. They have five children — Lovisa, 16, Reggie III, 9, Angela, 7, Dawn, 5, and Puyuk, 4. The caribou was shot by Joule; he eventually acquired the skill he needed to feed his family.

Along one wall are rows of trophies and a basket full of medals. There are plaques in a stack and other medals in frames on another wall. So many victories. Neither Joule, nor the history books of the Eskimo Indian Olympics have a complete count. He may have won 40 medals over the years. Maybe more. And then there are the Arctic Winter Games, the biennial festival of sport pitting teams from Alaskan and Canadian territories against one another. He won a bunch more in those competitions. The exact number doesn't matter. The meaning is clear. Their sheer volume speaks of greatness.

In the book *Heartbeat: World Eskimo Indian Olympics,* author Annabel Lund wrote that Joule "is the symbol, the ideal, the champion. He has been the shining example of the quintessential Eskimo athlete for over a decade."

She called him "Mr. Olympics."

Despite his triumphs and the obvious place of honor he gives his awards, Joule is somewhat embarrassed by this nickname. It is not that he is shy, not that he isn't proud, but the victories are a vehicle. Yes, he can raise his slight, 5-foot-6 body to incredible heights in the two-foot high kick. Yes, he has a big man's strength in those bulky forearms. But winning, you see, is not what it is about. Taking part is.

"If I could help one of my competitors win, I never felt that I lost," said Joule.

"What you do is help the other people to become their best."

That is the message of Reggie Joule the teacher. It is a message he has spread with warmth and sincerity to young people in schools across Alaska. He took his show on the road, to small villages, and to the biggest schools in Anchorage. He taught all the eager young listeners the story of his grandfather alerting the community of the success of the hunt by leaping in the air and thrusting out two feet. He taught them that the stick pull motion is the same as pulling a seal out of the ice. Partly because of Joule, Native sports are in physical education curricula in schools around the state.

"It's been brought out of the villages into the urban centers of Alaska through Reggie Joule," said Chris Anderson, general manager of the Eskimo Indian Olympics. "He was spreading culture and the spirit of cooperation. He's Mr. WEIO.

"One of the basic reasons the WEIO started back in 1961 was to share culture. The culture was dying. The culture is very much alive."

Very much alive in the young people who learned Native games not from family elders, but in their schools or from watching Joule.

"I learned from the other kids in school and they learned it from Reggie," said Carol Pickett, one of the greatest of World Eskimo Indian Olympics athletes.

Pickett, 26, lives in Fairbanks and now travels to give demonstrations and Native sports clinics herself. She grew up in Anchorage in an urban setting, with little knowledge of her family background. These days, though, she imparts the philosophy of Regie Joule.

"Reggie's teaching, it was important, or it (the heritage) would have been lost," said Pickett.

The first few times Pickett saw Native games being demonstrated, she didn't comprehend what was happening.

"I didn't know what was going on," she said. "I wasn't raised with it. I didn't learn the background (of the games) until a year or two later."

In competition, Joule "was the father-coach," said Pickett. "He'd tell us what we were doing wrong. He would help us out."

An infrequent visitor to the WEIO in his athletic old age, Joule has new pupils of Native games: his own kids. After dinner, Joule lay down on the carpeted floor of his living room, his arms stretched above his head. One by one, his youngest children stepped into his hands and he raised them up. They giggled at this play, but none fell. None bent his knees. They did not know it, but they already understood the principle of the blanket toss.

These days Joule is a busy man. He is a member of the NANA Development Corporation board of directors. He serves on government commissions on Native affairs and drug and alcohol abuse. Recently, he ran for the state legislature, but lost in the primary. In the summer, he operates the Suvuniguik Camp on the Kobuk River. The camp is for Eskimo teens and he teaches self-esteem as well as sports.

Joule is past his prime as an athlete and because of his commitment to the camp he did not participate in the Eskimo Indian Olympics between 1984 and 1988. In 1989, he went back and tried the blanket toss one more time. Had to. How could he come to the games and not play? The crowd would not have permitted it. Joule didn't place, but it didn't matter.

"I can look back with pride now," said Joule, "not only because I had something to do with it, but because of how it's being done.

"When I went back to Fairbanks and I saw those guys helping each other out in what ordinarily would be head-on competition, I knew I didn't need to be there. The next guys are going to be teaching it the same way. It's been institutionalized."

The master may be retired, but the teachings of the master remain.

George Attla
of North Pole

Mushing Legend Wise to Ways of Time

The old wise man walked from dog to dog with his stiff-legged gait. With each step, the leg tilted him to the left. The old wise man ladled liver broth onto metal plates and the dogs rattled their chains and yipped at his side.

The leg is no symbol of advancing age. It is more a symbol of stolen youth. It has been more than four decades since the leg bent.

The old wise man himself has never bent. Not to disease. Not to poverty. Not to other men. And, certainly, not to time. Not yet.

For most, time is the enemy of sure hands and bold thoughts. The old wise man knows time. The old wise man knows time ticks by in seconds and vanishes in years. But the old wise man knows this: men grow old and men grow wise by making time work for them.

As the eerie glow of a mid-day December sun illuminated the high, snow-coated branches of the tall spruce trees ringing his backyard in North Pole, George Attla, Jr., 56 years old, 56 years wise, and the greatest, most durable sprint dog musher who ever lived, did his chores.

"At this stage of my life," said Attla, "I know I can't beat time. Time is eventually going to beat me. But like anyone else, I'm fighting it."

He has fought time and beaten time for more than 30 years. For three decades, the Alaska winter has brought snow, cold, and George Attla victories.

By all measurements of sport, he has endured, survived and thrived. Read the resume. Ten Fur Rendezvous world championships. Eight North American championships. Wherever there has been a race—Anchorage, Fairbanks, Tok—he has won it. The foot-high trophy on his kitchen window sill commemorates his first major title, the Fur Rondy championship of 1958. 1958!

The athletes of 1958 included Mickey Mantle, Bill Russell, and Gordie Howe.

All are long retired, gone to their halls of fame. Do you plan to join them, George?

"People always ask," said Attla. "Why retire yet when you're almost on top of the sport? I think I'll retire when I don't think I can be competitive anymore."

Whatever year that is. During the 1988-89 season, Attla won the Su Valley Championship and finished second in the Orville Lake Memorial, the Exxon, the Fur Rendezvous, the North American, and the Tok Race of Champions. During the 1989-90 season, he picked up the odd title and earned a bunch more seconds. It is one thing to be active, to still be a participant at such an advanced athletic age, but to still be a threat? To still be a contender?

Retirement is the wrong question. Instead one should ask: Is George Attla forever?

Why shouldn't George Attla smirk at time? Many athletes retiring in their 30s say the legs go first. Some swear it's the eyes.

George's legs went first — at age 8.

Tuberculosis robbed years from his childhood. The illness ripped him from his home Athabascan village of Huslia, 260 miles northeast of Fairbanks, and confined him to hospitals three times for more than six years. Some of those hospitals were as far away as Sitka in the most distant part of the state. Doctors fused the bone in his right knee. He learned to live with it, to walk with it, to run with it.

The eyes went later, about 15 years ago. Tinted glasses hide eyes damaged by glaucoma.

In the 1978 movie of his life, "Spirit of the Wind," George's father sits by the side of his bed and says: "Men must sometimes face hard things."

Yes, Attla has faced the hard things. And ignored them. Yes, he has faced the pain. And willed himself beyond it. He has made it all work for him. At first, he was an unknown village boy with a limp and an Elvis Presley wave in his dark hair. No one else believed, so he whipped himself with anger.

"At the beginning, I wanted to be the best," said Attla. "I had to prove to myself I could do it."

For a long time, that was enough.

"In the middle years, it was just that I loved running dogs, being good at it and knowing I was good at it."

He proved himself again and again, year after year, place after place.

"From the very beginning, he was driven," said Eagle River musher Jim Welch. "He had some lifetime goals to establish, some landmarks. Ten world championships. I doubt if anyone is going to match that. He met all of those challenges. To say that he is fiercely competitive would be more than a mild understatement."

That is the other thing the middle-aged athlete loses — the edge. The hunger fades, the hunger is satiated. Lions who feast in the mid-day sun take respite yawning under shady trees.

This was Attla, too, for a brief period in the early 1980s. He ran the races hard, but coasted in training. The results were middling, but it didn't really hurt. He had done it all, hadn't he?

Fast Eddie Streeper's taunt in 1984 renewed him. Streeper, fresh in town, up from British Columbia, was a nonbeliever. Brash and bold, he represented the next generation yelling "Trail!"

Get out of the way, old man, Streeper said, you're washed up. The words stung. Old? OK, you can't deny birthdays, but finished? That was irreverent. Attla vowed to give him a spanking.

"In my mind, he put me down," said Attla. "I could do this thing (racing) and not be competitive and I don't think anyone has the right to tell me that kind of thing because of what I've done."

So he went out and beat Eddie, beat Eddie and answered all the doubters.

"You don't give George any excuse to be mad at you," said Welch. "Second place doesn't count for George. Someone saying, 'You're racing for second place,' you could see the fires just beginning to burn."

George Attla learned that he could never be content as a jogger, that he would always be in races for more than exercise, to win them.

"Yeah, I couldn't see it any other way," said Attla. "Everybody likes to win, don't they?"

It was 10 degrees and clear in the backyard, but Attla's hands were bare. He wore a beige snowmachine suit and strands of his thick mane of white hair poked out from under a cap bearing the name of his sponsor, Tesoro, the oil company. Occasionally, he stroked this thin stubble of gray and white beard. Leaning down, Attla fingered the sore paw of Treat, one of the dogs. Huskies are hardy, strong, and resilient. They can also be fragile. The dog had stepped in a hole and injured a small foot bone.

"That's the weakest link in a dog," said Attla.

The best dog mushers need the best dogs, or they must somehow make their dogs the best. The musher must know the dogs, read the dogs. Spotting talent in any sport is no science; it's a very imprecise art.

In a 1974 book, *Everything I Know About Training and Racing Sled Dogs,* written with Bella Levorsen, Attla recounts a time he traveled all over Alaska looking for dogs. He saw some 500 animals and rejected them before choosing to buy one. He couldn't explain why that one seemed special or why the others did not please him.

But he did make very clear his feelings about who is the brains of the racing outfit, who must live with any failures.

"The dog never makes a mistake," wrote Attla. "He is just a dog and he does what he does because he is a dog and thinks like a dog. It is you that makes the mistake because you haven't trained him to do what you want him to do when you want him to do it."

There is not a lot of romance in that description, but there is a sense of responsibility and a very specific outlook: no excuses.

Each October Attla begins running his dogs hard, readying them for the winter grind. Beginning the 1990 sprint dog season, he had 80 dogs, many of them pups. Of those, some 26 formed the pool of racers for the coming months.

Attla has always had the gift to make dogs do things his way and respond to his commands. Over the years, a dozen, perhaps, have been special—Nellie and Tuffy, Blue and Johnny, Jarvi and Scottie and others—all leaders. They all had speed, savvy, and an intangible that is hard to measure in old, wise men and young, frisky dogs.

"The desire to win," said Attla. "They all had that."

And Attla brought it out.

"He can do things with dogs no one else can do," Welch said. "He has the ability to understand dogs so well and get in their heads so well he can get the last ounce of ability they have.

"Dogs can't speak. Huskies are the toughest dog and among the toughest creatures on earth. They don't whine and they don't moan and groan. To be able to understand them and to be able to do something about it is an art. George Attla is the Pablo Picasso of dog mushing."

Attla walked around his dog yard, the broth sloshing in a bucket, the bucket banging against his knee. He stopped and patted the belly of one dog.

"They're a little bit fat now," he said. "You want their ribs showing. To the general public, they look starved."

To the general public, Attla himself still looks starved. He is as slender as ever—there are just 155 pounds for his dogs to tote down the trail—and after finally realizing his hunger to win is everlasting, he no longer grows weary of solving the puzzle of making new dogs fit with old dogs.

"Each dog has its own personality," said Attla. "No two dogs can be handled alike to accomplish the same purpose. There's no end to it. It's like meeting new people. There's always a new crop of pups. You have to figure their minds."

Sitting at the kitchen table, sipping coffee and smoking a cigarette, Attla is surrounded by memorabilia. Trophies are clustered so thick on a shelf that it is a wonder it does not collapse. Hanging on one wall of the living room is a framed proclamation from the Alaska Legislature congratulating Attla on his 30th year as a musher.

The past is everywhere, reminders of what he has done, how many winters have passed. But it is the future which teases Attla, the winters to come, that intrigue him.

The 1988-89 season was a good one, a grand season, with high finishes and prize money every week. A good season for anyone but George Attla. The 1989-90 season was not quite as good, but quite respectable. The first year, though, Roxy Wright of Salcha won the triple crown — the Fur Rondy, the North American, and Tok, too. The next year, Charlie Champaine, her husband, won the triple crown, driving the same dogs. So that is why Attla calls it only a fair year. To listen to him is to listen to Vince Lombardi. Winning is the only thing.

"I'm looking for better things," said Attla.

That's what he looks for in his futures. To find better things, that means selling dogs and buying dogs. Thirteen of the 26 racing dogs were new for the 1990 winter campaign. Moses, one of the leaders, was kept. Grace, one of the other leaders, was sold.

"I gambled on it," said Attla. "I thought, 'I got to get rid of Grace to get better.' When you get older you start thinking about your next move. You're always trying to take shortcuts to do the same thing."

Attla lives in the Interior where the winter can bring temperatures of minus 60 or colder. But he is a poker player who plays cards cautiously, who sometimes seems to be trying to lull his opponents to dismiss him only as an old man even as he rebuts them.

In one of the first races of the 1990 season, Attla finished in second place in the Orville Lake Memorial in Anchorage. A week before he'd finished second in the season-opening Su Valley Championship. It was hard to take Attla too seriously when he complained of the cold in Anchorage. Even if old bones do stiffen when it's minus 10, this is a man who should be used to it. Attla did sit in his truck until just before start time.

When he stepped on the runners of his sled and the dogs whooshed away from the starting line at the Tudor Track, a fur pony tail bounced on the back of Attla's blue, fur-trimmed parka.

Attla finished the first heat swiftly, pleased that another new leader — Sue — had meshed well with Moses. But he lay in sixth place. The season before, Attla usually led early and got caught at the end.

"It almost looked as if the dogs needed to be tougher," he said.

Sunday the second day, Attla's dogs were tougher than most. They had the second-fastest second heat time and that pulled him into second place. Perhaps he had taught old dogs new tricks? No matter, really. The Orville Lake is for experimenting. The long races, Attla's specialty, were coming later, and other mushers didn't doubt he would be there for the big ones. Attla has always used the shorter, 10-mile early-season races for experimentation. He only cares about the big ones.

"Maybe when I'm older, I'll know one-quarter of what he knows," said Champaine, 40, of Salcha. "You'll see George when we get to the 14-mile and 16-mile races."

Or the 20-mile ones. There is no shortcut up Cordova Hill — the last uphill mile in the world championship race in Anchorage each February — and that stretch of ground has never seemed longer to an Attla trotting alongside the sled. But if the race is always to the swiftest, it is not always to the fittest. You can be young and foolish, or you can be old and wise. Knowing the dogs, knowing the trail, knowing the distance, all count.

"There are a lot of things actually involved besides the physical part," said Gareth Wright, a man who should know.

Wright, 61, won the North American in 1950 and again in 1983. He raced sprint dogs for 42 years and jokingly said that gives him the right to call Attla "a babe in the woods yet." Although his daughter is Attla's main rival, Wright believes Attla can be a winner again.

"That's his career. That's his whole life," said Wright. "George doesn't even look any different except his hair got whiter."

Doesn't look different, doesn't think different. There is always something to prove. If not now, soon. If not soon, sooner or later.

"I want to win the Rendezvous when I'm 60," said Attla.

He chuckled when he said it, but he was serious.

"Well, good luck to him," Wright said. "Anything you believe in, it's possible to do. He's a very dedicated man and he's a stubborn man."

Still, 60? Wouldn't that be something? Everyone knows which races Attla cares about.

"What the hell," said Attla. "You never quit dreaming. There's no end to dreaming. There's always something else to shoot for."

Always something for old wise men to chase as the seconds tick off. Somehow, you think, George Attla will still stir the wind once more with his spirit.